M000239558

Anjila,

Thank you so much
for opening your heart
& life stories.

Blessings,

Anamarie Seidel
&
Amy Seidel

REGISTER THIS BOOK!

Visit our website to receive your free S.T.E.P.s
PlayBook which contains all the exercises in this book
and additional unpublished content. You will also
receive exclusive access to articles, videos and mp3s
only available to our customers.

Go to

WWW.PARENTOUTLOUD.COM/STEP

passcode: WYDFYKI

Advance Praise

for

What You Don't Fix... Your Kids Inherit

"Unlike other parenting books weighed down with obscure clinical jargon, the Seidels speak with passion and authenticity, drawing upon their experience as parents of four to address the often overlooked areas such as the mental and emotional traits one has to exhibit while parenting. Through a series of compelling analogies and images, the Seidels take readers through this transformation posing powerful questions to help the reader pinpoint unhealthy beliefs and habits while providing the steps to quickly and easily change them."

— Sylvia Coleman, BA, CMT,
Author of *Creating a New Normal, TheSylviaSite.com*

"What will your legacy be? What will be different because you were born and you lived? Anamarie and Cory Seidel say 'What we don't fix our children will inherit.' Hmmm...think about that. Wow! Decide that you are going to play a role in creating a brighter tomorrow on this day by the choices you make. Get out of your head and into your greatness."

— Les Brown
Motivational Speaker, Author, Coach, *LesBrown.com*

"I have worked with teens and their families for over 15 years. I wish Anamarie and Cory had written this book years ago so I could have recommended it to my clients. Every parent should read and follow the wisdom in this book!"

— Anne Pustil, B.Sc., M.Ed.,
Therapist and Coach, *CoachingInANutshell.com*

"What a great book! I've taught people for years about limiting beliefs and how to get rid of them, yet in all that time, no one I've come across has ever equated it to the effect your beliefs have on your kids! This really is a MUST read for all parents because not only do your kids inherit your DNA (which medical science can now demonstrate contains your beliefs), they also receive the vast majority of their learned behavior from you that will set them up for the rest of their lives. If you want to improve the quality of your kids' lives, the single biggest thing you can do for them is get rid of your limiting beliefs, which this book can help you do."

— **Karen Dimmick**, CHt,
Creator of *EnlightenedMillionaireCode.com*

"The Seidels have hit a home run with this book! If you want your children to excel not just in Little League but in Life, you owe it to yourself to get this book and give it to every parent and grandparent you know. The principles that Anamarie and Cory teach are timeless, and will help both you and your children reach their full life potential beyond what you ever thought possible. As a loving father and family man myself, I've used these techniques to transform my own children. Listen to the Seidels; seek out their wisdom, and swing for the fence!"

— **Dave Albano**, MBA,
Author, Speaker, Results Coach, *FullLifePotential.com*

"Through their book, What You Don't Fix ... Your Kids Inherit, Anamarie and Cory Seidel provide the answers parents have been asking for. Their brilliant and creative analogies are woven throughout the chapters to help parents finally gain a true understanding of how the law of attraction works and how it can be implemented into the everyday lives of every family."

— **Denny Hagel**,
Author of *Mini-Me Syndrome, MissingSecretToParenting.com*

"As a leading authority on creating wealth today, and a father of four beautiful children, I can affirm that many of these concepts are not only great for our children, but more importantly, they are essential for us to apply as parents. Living by these principles will not only help us acquire riches, it will help us leave a legacy."

— **Chris Miles**,
Financial Coach, *FireYourFinancialAdvisor.com*

WHAT
YOU DON'T FIX...

YOUR KIDS INHERIT

Change Your Habits, Improve Their World

ANAMARIE & CORY SEIDEL

.

BOUND
PUBLISHING

All Rights Reserved
© 2010 by Anamarie and Cory Seidel, Six-S Solutions

This book may not be reproduced in whole or in part, by any means, without written consent of the publisher.

BOUND PUBLISHING

United States	Canada
6501 E. Greenway Pkwy	Suite 114
#103-480	720 28th St. NE
Scottsdale, AZ 85254	Calgary, AB T2A 6R3

Toll Free Phone & Fax: 1-888-237-1627
Email: info@boundpublishing.com
Web: www.BoundPublishing.com
ISBN: 978-0-9867762-3-6

Library of Congress Control Number: 2010943478

Cover Design: Anamarie Seidel, Finely Finished, LLC
Hand Models: Anamarie, Cory, Justine and Dane Seidel
Paper Sculpture Tools: Anamarie Seidel
Blueprints: Courtesy of Tovani Architects
Cover Photography: www.JimTobin.com
Photography: www.Jennea.com
White Guy Images: www.JesterArtsIllustrations.com
Text: Anamarie Seidel, Finely Finished, LLC
Edit: Lynda Masterson, Valyn Enterprises, LLC

COMPANIES, ORGANIZATIONS, INSTITUTIONS, AND INDUSTRY PUBLICATIONS. Quantity discounts are available on bulk purchases of this book for reselling, educational purposes, subscription incentives, gifts, sponsorship, or fundraising. Special books or book excerpts can also be created to fit specific needs such as private labeling with your logo on the cover and a message from a VIP printed inside. For more information, please contact our Special Sales Department at Bound Publishing.

DEDICATION

We dedicate this book to our five children; In Heaven and on Earth: Tyler, Justine, Andrew, Dane, Bradley, who bring us joy and inspiration daily. You have enhanced our lives immeasurably. Thank you.

Through our journey of personal growth, we hope to pass on what we've learned in order to make a difference for the future generations of the world.

FOREWORD

Albert Schweitzer said something really interesting. He said, "Example is not the main thing in influencing others; it is the only thing." We have got to set an example for our children. We've got to be decisive and live the way we want to live. Our children are individualized expressions of life. Each one is unique with great potential. They are not from us, but through us. Our children are an extension of us. We programmed them. Their programming is usually complete before they are six years old. If they go in the wrong direction, it's because we've steered them in the wrong direction.

I've been teaching people about the power of their mind for over forty years and know with absolute certainty that, until we rid ourselves of our limiting beliefs, we will perpetuate a cycle of destructive thought processes in future generations. We all have the potential for greatness. Several years ago I wrote *You Were Born Rich*, which is based on the idea that abundance is yours already; you only have to choose it. I find an amazing parallel between this book and Anamarie and Cory Seidel's *What You Don't Fix ... Your Kids Inherit* in that it teaches parents to change their mindset in order to prevent their limiting beliefs from infiltrating their children's minds.

I believe the most important lesson we can teach our children is to *make decisions*. If you can choose your happiness, then you can also choose to give your children the knowledge to create a better life for themselves. Anamarie and Cory are proactive parents who are leading their children in a very powerful direction on how they can achieve lifelong success and happiness by choosing their path according to the Natural Laws of the Universe.

What You Don't Fix ... Your Kids Inherit teaches parents to evaluate their current parenting techniques. Anamarie and Cory show us, in very simple terms, that we can raise our children following nature's Universal Laws. It is simply a matter of being aware of and knowing how the Universe operates and then applying this knowledge to your parenting. True self-discovery, self-knowledge, and the proper instruction in applying the Intellectual Faculties will help anyone achieve their lifelong goals. Success, therefore, is within the reach of every aspiring person, both parents and children.

I encourage you to not only read this book, but to actually apply the wisdom contained within to achieve a balanced family life and well adjusted, happy children. Start working with nature and give your children a solid foundation upon which to build.

–Bob Proctor

Bestselling Author, Professional Speaker, and Chairman of LifeSuccess Productions

INTRODUCTION

There is a moment in the life of all parents when they look at the amazing child they have brought into this world, who used to be so cute, so tiny, and so precious when born, and who is now having a major meltdown. That parent sighs in frustration and says, "If only there was a guidebook on raising children." *What You Don't Fix ... Your Kids Inherit* is not that kind of manual. Instead, it is something far more powerful. This book will help you discover the power you have within yourself to be, do, and have anything you want. We give you the tools to build that self awareness in you and your children.

One of the most important metaphors that we learned is the story of how Chinese bamboo grows. It is a very fragile and slow-growing plant that averages only two inches a year only if it is nurtured and really watched over. So even if the bamboo is meticulously cared for, it only grows eight inches in four years. This may not seem like much progress, but what most people don't realize is that in the fifth year it grows over eighty feet! In many ways, our children are much like the bamboo plant. Over the first four years, much more happens to our children than appears on the surface. During those early years, a massive root system, their belief system, is being established that will carry them throughout the rest of their lives.[38]

As you read *What You Don't Fix ... Your Kids Inherit*, you will start on a journey that is much like the growing of the Chinese bamboo. "Sometimes, it feels like we're studying, practicing, remembering, putting our focus on feeling with our hearts, and opening our minds, yet it hardly seems as though anything is changing. But then, all of a sudden, feels as if our entire lives have moved to a whole new level."[39] The majority of parents agree their children are the most important part of their lives, so why then do we spend more time training for our careers, looking for new hobbies, or even watching television than learning how to give our children the tools for success? A mother of seven once said, "The love is instinctual but the skills are not." In *What You Don't Fix ... Your Kids Inherit*, we don't focus on what parents are doing wrong or right; instead, we want to share the valuable knowledge we have learned through our own personal growth journey. Each chapter in this book provides new options for parents and encourages them to teach their children though love, example, following the Natural Laws of the Universe, and expanding the Higher Facilities of their minds.

If we look at how much time and money we spend at sporting events, sitting in front of the television, restaurants, and vacations, compared with what we spend on parenting education, we'll see just how little we invest in our children's futures. *What You Don't Fix ... Your Kids Inherit* is your personal toolbox from which you can take what you need to change your life, and in turn, change the beliefs your children inherit. This book is an investment in your personal growth, your child's future, and in future generations.

Start today and take time to nurture that which is real—our children. Take time to plant thoughts that are kind and loving about yourself and your children. You'll notice over time a dramatic improvement in your children's behavior and a more meaningful relationship. You'll look back and say, "This is a whole new life; how did this happen?" Well, it happened a little at a time ... and all at once. How are you spending your time? Are you making the world a better place for your children or letting time slip through your fingers?

What You Don't Fix ... Your Kids Inherit will challenge, inspire, and guide you into a new chapter in the relationship with your children. Hopefully, you'll also smile a bit and laugh at some of the events that have occurred. We most certainly have done this while going through our own processes. Not taking life so seriously and the having the ability to laugh at yourself is a liberating way to live. Now, are you ready to get started?

-Anamarie and Cory Seidel

CONTENTS

8. Flipping the Switch

We'll show you how much better your life will be with a positive attitude and how you can rewire your mindset and change your vibration. You'll discover a list of all the things that make you happy and pick from the list when you are feeling cranky. Exercise and music really helps kids change their vibe. We need to define our attitude and we need to help our children *learn the words* that define their attitudes. How often do we tell our kids to go to their room until they can change their attitude, but we never teach them *what* attitude is or how to change it?

9. The Final Inspection

Now that you know that you can change your thought process and vibration, we'll go through every aspect of your life and look at the different methods to use the previous information to give you everything you want in life. Goals are important, but how do we teach our children to accomplish them? Simple: through Goal Cards and Vision Boards … perhaps Mind Movies for the computer-savvy kids. Gratitude will also be a focus of this chapter as well as learning to receive the good in your life.

10. Landscaping

In this chapter, we'll discuss the value of money and how to earn money at any age. You can live an abundantly green life through multiple sources of income. It is possible to make money at any age. Everyone deserves to have money—riches are for everyone. It's okay to want to have money, contrary to what religion and society teaches. We'll show you how to be innovative and creative to expand your financial future.

CHAPTER 1

SURVEY THE SCENE

*One generation plants the trees;
another gets the shade.*

—Chinese proverb

"Why do we cut the ends off of the roast every Sunday?" Sandy asked her mother, as she peeled a potato.

"Because Grandma always did," her mother replied, placing the roast into a pan with plenty of room for a variety of vegetables.

"How come?"

The mother was rather perplexed since no one had ever asked her that question before. She had prepared the same Sunday family dinner of roast beef, mashed potatoes, and apple pie for as long as she could remember.

"Well sweetie, I really don't know the answer to your question." She smiled. "Your grandma always cut the ends off of her roast and she taught me how to cook. I never ever wondered why. Let's call Grandma and ask her why she cuts the roast that way."

Sandy quickly grabbed the phone and dialed. "Grandma, Mom and I were just wondering why you cut the ends of the roast before you put it in the pan."

There was a pause. "Because your grandfather's favorite food is roast beef and that is all he wanted to eat when we were first married. Money was very tight and I didn't have a pan big enough to fit an entire roast so I had to chop off the ends to make it fit."

Your Viewpoint

Children come into this world with their conscious and subconscious minds completely blank, like an empty canvas. We, as parents, are the most influential people in their lives and consequently paint their canvas with our beliefs. Because our beliefs become theirs, we need to excavate any unrealistic or sabotaging thoughts before we pass them on to our children. Do you want to imprison your children with your fears, or give them the gift of knowing that they can be anything they want in this world? So often we say things about our children such as he's lazy, she's smart, he's stubborn, or she's the comic, but we must be careful about this because these thoughts help to establish a paradigm and build their reality.[5]

> Paradigms are the governing belief systems that determine our success in life and as a parent.

Paradigms are the governing belief systems that determine our success in life and as a parent. We learned many of our paradigms from our parents, which is why it is so important to change the beliefs that aren't serving us, so that we don't pass them on to our children.[5] Being a parent is one of the most rewarding experiences in life. The joy our children bring to our lives is, at times, inexplicable. When your child's canvas is colored with positive, powerful beliefs, imagine the life they can create!

To regain control of our thoughts and beliefs, we have to look at our past and see how we were raised. Did your parents bicker about money and live with a mindset of never having enough, or did they look at problems as opportunities in disguise? When children are surrounded in positive, loving, and caring environments, they turn out to be positive, caring and loving themselves. Kids need that type of a support network. The majority of parents want their children to have a better life than they had, but unfortunately, some weren't raised in a supportive environment and continue to pass those negative beliefs onto their children. We cannot attempt to change someone else, including our own kids, if we don't change ourselves first. It has to start with parents.[5]

Most parents get caught in a rut and continue to raise their children the same way they were raised. We made the decision to parent our children differently from how we were parented, and for us, the only way to do so was through personal development. If you stop, take time to reflect about who you are, take an honest look at yourself, and really try to understand what is going on, your life will improve tenfold. As we mature, certain beliefs are ingrained in us. For example, if your mother was a germaphobe, and every five minutes she not only washed her hands but yours as well, you may very well take that belief into your adulthood, causing you to have hand sanitizer in every nook and cranny of your home, office, and car. The good news is that we can shift our paradigms to create a new and healthy way of thinking and acting. Just think about how much of a positive effect this would have on our children!

Many of the thoughts we think every day are not ours. We know this sounds strange, but the majority of our present-day thoughts didn't originate in our own minds. Instead, they are the offspring of those around us, or they have been passed down from generation to generation.[5] As parents, it is important for us to realize that our children are incredible and unique. We are responsible for molding these young minds and melding them into the people they ultimately become. Stop and think about what an enormous responsibility this is. Our children are one of the best gifts to the world, which is why it is so important to create a paradigm shift. We literally shape the way they spend the rest of their lives by programming their minds. These programs are what they'll use to relate to the world as they continue to grow. We need to be aware of their genius and have respect for them as individuals. This knowledge has allowed us to let our kids grow in their own way as well as to nurture them along their journey.

> *Our paradigms control our current behaviors and lives. Change them and you can change your life!*

Perform the Survey

Before you can build a structure, you must have a complete survey performed. How else are you going to find the best location for your dream home or your new office? The same is true for your life. Think back to the story about the roast at the beginning of this chapter. If something as simple as cutting off the ends of a roast to fit in a pan can be passed down from generation to generation, then can you imagine what else can be misconstrued? How many outdated paradigms do you have in your life? Are you building your house on sand because you failed to do a survey?

Let's say, for example, you grew up in home where your parents lived paycheck to paycheck. Your parents' arguments and feelings of never having enough were ingrained in you and still haunt you today. As a child, you remember saying to yourself, "There is no way I'm going to live this way. When I grow up I'm going to be rich." Fast forward twenty-five years: you want to create a family budget in order to build an emergency expense fund because you're tired of scrambling for money every time your air conditioner breaks or you need a new set of tires. You tell yourself, "This time it is going to be different. I'm going to save ten percent of every paycheck." The first two months you did exactly as planned and carefully set aside that ten percent. The third month, however, was not so good; with the money you did save, you decided to buy a new flat screen TV for the basement. Now, you're back in the same spending habits with no emergency fund, and you're upset with yourself. How much of an effect do you think your upbringing had to do with this scenario?

Our children are an extension of us and if we don't like their behavior, we need to start by looking at ourselves.

With the example above, we see that it can be a difficult process to change habitual thinking patterns that have been instilled since our childhood. More often than not, people are unhappy and lack fulfillment because they don't know how to unlearn their outdated beliefs. In some cases, they may not even understand what the problem is. To break free from these self-sabotaging thought processes, we have to take an internal survey and question everything we've been taught. As small children, the thoughts of our parents, teachers, ministers, and any other influential people became our own. During our youth, we looked to those closest to us for guidance, and, as a result, we took on their beliefs. Unfortunately, many times the majority of these thoughts are limiting, in that they prevent us from finding what truly makes us happy. These distorted thoughts sabotage our own happiness because we're living according to someone else's values and opinions. More importantly, however, we have to consider who else our distorted thoughts are affecting: our children.[5]

Before the Grading

Many parents make parenting something that it's not. Our children are an extension of us, and if we don't like their behavior, we need to start by looking at ourselves. As parents, we only want what's best for our children and to have the happiest life possible, but have you ever wondered what limiting beliefs you unknowingly pass on to your children? The first six years of your child's life, are very influential. During this time, you have to build a foundation for them because in those formative years, they are ingrained with the mindset they will carry for the rest of their lives; this affects how they interact with the world and everything in it.[5] But what if you're reading this and all of your children are older than six years? We have found with our children that *it is never too late to start!* We started teaching the content in this book to Justine when she was ten years old and it's amazing how her attitude and behavior has changed for the better.

> **The first six years of your child's life, are very influential because that is when they are ingrained with the mindset they carry for the rest of their lives.**

"All of your actions, words, and thoughts count when you are a parent. We don't have the luxury of thinking, 'Well, I've got tomorrow,' or 'I've got more time.' Every decision you make affects something in your child's life, which is why it is imperative that you are mindful of the decisions you make during their formative years."[10]

> *You can, at this very moment, make a conscious effort to change your thoughts and give your children a lasting legacy of happiness and security.*

"Today's culture places a great deal of pressure on our youth. Movies, television, and even school have placed unrealistic expectations on our kids. Each day they walk into a world full of negativity and bad influences. Once they enter into environments such as school, they're subject to many outside influences that are beyond your control. They learn good and bad habits and face difficult decisions, many of which they aren't equipped to handle.

We want to help our kids, but unfortunately, many parents who try to help end up making things worse. This isn't because parents don't care, but because they do not know how to rid themselves of their own self-destructive thoughts."[4] Think about the ramifications of this. Your children inherit these thoughts from you and then pass them on to their children, who pass them on to their children, and so on, and so on ... this becomes a vicious cycle. But it doesn't have to. If, however, you give them a strong foundation, they will have the confidence to make the right decisions. In the next two chapters, we're going to help you understand how to create your own paradigm shift so you can give them the firm foundation they need to succeed in this world.

ACTION STEPS

1. Make a list of beliefs you inherited from your parents or grandparents that you would like to change. (We'll show you how to change them in later chapters.)

2. Make a list of negative words you use to describe yourself.

3. Make a list negative words your children use to describe themselves.

For more writing space please visit
www.ParentOutLoud.com/STEP to download your free PlayBook.

CHAPTER 2

EXCAVATION

*Knowing yourself is the beginning
of all wisdom.*

–Aristotle

"Mom, school starts tomorrow and I have to have my big crayon box. Have you seen them? I can't find them." Justine continued to wander in a haphazard fashion through the living room. She had been looking all over the house for a bright yellow box of 96 Crayola Crayons.

"Where have you looked?" Anamarie said.

"Everywhere. I've looked in my room, in the red room, the living room, the kitchen and the TV room. Everywhere, and I just can't find them."

Anamarie smiled because she knew the box was sitting on a shelf at her daughter's eye level in a bookcase in the living-room. "Walk straight ahead and look."

Justine was about two feet from the bookcase, looked straight ahead, up, down and then at her mother intensely, "Where? They're not here. I can't find them!"

"Just look straight ahead."

"Mom, they are not here."

"Justine, you are going to laugh soon. I want you to now tell yourself that you can find your crayons."

She paused, changed her thought, looked ahead and gasped. "Those were not there before!" She kept looking at Anamarie and then back to the bookcase and started to laugh. "They were invisible! Those were not there before!"

Anamarie laughed, "This is the most perfect example of whatever you tell yourself, your brain will make you right. If you can't, you're right. If you can, you're right. It is so important to tell your brain what you can do."

Higher Quality Tools

Now that you've seen the impact parenting has on the perpetuation of beliefs; both good and bad, let's dig a little deeper into how those beliefs are created. We're going to look at the two parts of your mind; conscious and subconscious. Just how do they work together to create our perceptions, behaviors and habits? We'll also show you two different visual images to help you understand the thought, feeling, action, and results cycle.

President Lincoln's famous speech, noted for the phrase "a house divided against itself cannot stand," is significant in that he was referring to the importance of the country standing together and presenting a united front. The same is true for a family. For a family to grow strong, it has to have a foundation of solid beliefs. We need to build our house on realistic, encouraging, and productive beliefs so that when we pass them onto our children, they can stand on their own in this world. A family must be one tight unit, not two; it's not the parents versus the children. Family members need to feel that their home is a sanctuary from outside life. As you may have noticed when you read the contents page, a running theme throughout this book is the house analogy. We chose this analogy because just like a home that is continuously maintained to keep from falling to ruin, our minds must be maintained and cared for as well. Our mind is powerful and has intrigued scholars and scientists for thousands of years. It holds the key to unlock the door to unlimited potential and can help us to live in a house full of prosperity and abundance.

Family members need to feel that their home is a sanctuary from outside life.

Which Level Do You Live On?

Before we go any further, we would first like to point out that we are going to start getting into some really deep concepts. It's not every day that we focus on understanding how our mind works and why we *do, say and think* the things we do. It is important to know how your beliefs are created in order to rewrite new beliefs that will help you change your life.

The majority of people use the terms brain and mind interchangeably. The two, however, are very different. Our brain is an organ that is part of our central nervous system. It is the control center of the body that enables us to learn, feel, and move. Our mind, on the other hand, encompasses every cell of our body and is responsible for our higher functions such as reasoning, thought, and memory and has the capability to expand beyond our physical body. It is part of the infinite energy of the Universe.[5]

So how does your mind expand beyond your body? Have you ever felt like you were being watched and turned to find out that someone was indeed staring at you? That was their mind reaching out to you with laser precision, and you felt that connection without using your eyes. What does your mind look like? Do you have a picture? Most people envision a picture of a brain. Our mind looks nothing like the grey head of cauliflower we've all seen in textbooks.

Unfortunately, the mind is something abstract and cannot be easily pictured. When was the last time you had to describe a difficult concept to your child? Was it easier to fumble over the words or take out a box of crayons and draw out a picture? Or, if you have older kids, did you search the Internet to find a descriptive image?[5]

> One day we were trying to explain how the mind worked to our daughter, Justine, for the umpteenth time, and we finally decided to draw her a picture. After we used the diagram, she said, "Why didn't you show me that before? It makes sense to me now." Just as children think in pictures, so do adults.

Think about your last family outing for a moment. What did you see? Did you see a scrolling marquee of words describing the outing? No, instead you probably saw a mental image; like a movie on the screen of your mind as if you were enjoying a family video.

No matter what topic you are asked about, an image immediately flashes in your head. For us to have a true understanding of the mind, and because our thoughts are visual, we must have a clear, vivid image of our mind. Below is a seemingly simplistic drawing, yet it is one of the most powerful and important pictures you'll ever need to help you understand our minds and how we think. Our mentor, Bob Proctor, showed us this image, which was created by Dr. Thurman Fleet. We, in turn, shared it with our children and now would like to do the same with you. Keep in mind that this picture is a tool to release your paradigms and give your children a firm foundation for their future.[5]

The image of the Stickman brings order and understanding to your mind by giving you a picture that you can visualize. Notice the two levels: the Conscious and the Subconscious Minds. This image explains how each level of your mind works together with your body to give you your results in life. Remember, our children are just little human beings who lack life experiences and depend on us to teach them. When we understand our own mind and train it to think in the correct manner as well, we can maximize the infinite power within our children's magnificent young minds. When you share this image with your children as we did, it teaches them how their thoughts create their reality. By changing their thoughts, they can create the life they desire.[5]

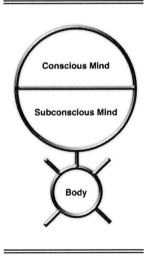

Stickman Image

In most cases, all of an individual's conscious attention focuses on the physical aspect of their lives. We exercise to lose weight, for instance, yet we don't change our eating habits. What type of an example does this set for our kids? All of our bodily experiences are an expression of our mind. Notice on the drawing that the head of the Stickman is noticeably larger than the body, indicating that our mind, not our body, is dominant over our lives. In order for us to promote productive thoughts in our children, we must have a clear and concise understanding of how our minds work, so let's take the picture above and discuss each section individually.[5]

The Conscious Mind

Also known as the thinking mind, *free will* resides in our conscious mind. It can accept or reject any idea.[5] Think about how quickly children form beliefs. How many adults don't like dogs because a dog jumped on them as a young child and scared them half to death? Because of that one incident, they believe that all dogs are going to hurt them. Unless one takes the time to examine this belief, they're going to live with this irrational fear their entire life.

The conscious mind also reads and interprets the stimuli taken in from our five senses: sound, sight, taste, touch, and smell. Because we think in pictures, anytime one or all of our five senses is triggered, we instantly create a picture in our mind. This is much like an antennae or satellite dish that transmits signals to your television set. Your conscious mind is the gateway through which external stimuli travel to your subconscious mind. Certain feelings occur depending on the interpretation you give to these external stimuli. Does the smell of fresh baked apple pie take you back in time to Sunday dinners? What about the feel of the pine needles on a Christmas tree? What about the time you found a

Free-will resides in our conscious mind. It can accept or reject any idea.

new bicycle or red wagon under the tree? Do you feel positive or negative energy in your body? As these memories come to you, your conscious mind actually has the power to accept the thoughts and feelings from your subconscious that you want to keep. If you don't like the feelings, you can reject the thoughts and change them ... but only if you know how.[5]

The Subconscious Mind

Our subconscious has no ability to reject any idea or thought; it simply accepts every suggestion made to it. Each thought you have is impressed upon the subconscious part of your mind. It can't discriminate any information and takes in all the information it receives as facts. All of those words, actions, and behaviors of your parents, teachers, clergy, coaches, and any other early mentors, were taken in through your conscious mind and embedded into your subconscious mind.[5]

> **Our subconscious has no ability to reject any idea or thought; it simply accepts every suggestion made to it.**

Your conscious mind gathers thoughts and filters them down into your subconscious mind where they bounce around and try to mix with your beliefs. If your beliefs are in alignment and mix with the thoughts, like coffee and cream, then you feel fine. If those thoughts are not in alignment with your beliefs, like oil and vinegar, conflict starts happening. No matter how hard you try to stir them together, they will not mix. This results in uncomfortable feelings like sadness, frustration or anger. Your body is the instrument reflecting the activity happening in your mind. If you don't like how you're feeling, you have to go back and look at the thoughts and beliefs that are making you feel that way.[5]

Thought→Feeling→Result Cycle

To better explain, let's look at a real life example.

> Our children give us a beautiful card. Our conscious mind (through our eyes) reads and interprets the words; this information then moves into our subconscious mind and we feel how much our children love us. This feeling then migrates into our body, and we are happy. This type of emotion changes the vibration in every cell of our body; we radiate happiness, and others want to be around our uplifting energy.

The Body

Although it may not seem like it, the body is only a small presentation of ourselves to the world. This is the smallest portion of the Stickman. It is only an instrument of the mind and is an outward appearance to the world. However, without the body, the mind can't act upon its beliefs. Every thought moves through your two minds and then your subconscious turns it into emotions, which are then expressed through your body as your feelings. The thoughts that enter your mind are either in harmony or disharmony with your beliefs, which affects your emotions. This is where the body comes in to play. You feel the emotions in your body and, being the instrument of your mind, your body moves into action based on what your mind tells it to do. Your body is what interacts with your environment. Then, when your body takes action in the environment, you get a reaction. (Remember Newton's Law of Motion—for every action, there is an opposite and equal reaction!) It is this action-reaction that gives you your results. So, the body is used by the mind to interact with the environment around us, which enables us to get the results we receive in our lives.[5]

> *A child is born with empty conscious and subconscious minds. A child's subconscious mind is like a sponge. It soaks up everything, good and bad, with which it comes into contact.*

A Habit Schematic

Let's go back and look at the subconscious a bit more and you'll realize how much it controls our daily lives. Our subconscious mind is a culmination of our past experiences and memories. It is also where our habits and belief systems are formed. It consists of memories, which have an emotional connection to the past: this is the primary reason it can be so difficult to discontinue any limiting beliefs and behaviors. Consider it a storage unit for all that has happened in our lives. It is quite similar to our childhood home in that it is also where our memories are stored. What we feel, think, or do forms the basis of our experiences, which are stored in the form of underlying impressions in the subconscious mind. These perceptions cause us to behave or think in certain ways.[5]

Teach your children that they can do anything they want to do, that they can accomplish anything they want to accomplish.

The subconscious drives our mind in the same way a locomotive pulls the cargo cars down the track. It works nonstop, twenty-four hours a day, fueling our thoughts. This process occurs subconsciously and is so rapid that our feelings prompt our behavior. It is so automatic to us that we don't even have time to notice it is happening. Almost instantaneously, we react when we hear or see something.

> Every time Cory and I saw an ambulance, for instance, we thought of our firstborn child. The flashing lights and sirens transported us back to the time when our son passed away of SIDS. We made a conscious decision to change and reprogram that habit because the feeling of sadness and loss that the ambulance triggered wasn't serving us anymore. It was just causing us to re-live our grief.

Our beliefs that are stored in our subconscious mind are expressed through our actions, which are visible to our children. Kids do as they see, not as they are told, and your limiting beliefs can filter into their adult lives and cause problems. If you want to know what you are thinking subconsciously, simply look at the results in your child's life.[5] Many times, parents don't think about their reactions consciously. Just as we made a conscious decision to change our reaction to the sounds of sirens and sight of flashing lights, you need to look at your actions and do the same.

"Your subconscious mind is the part of you that controls all the programming of your habits. Think of it as software for the mind; it's running all of your programs. To change our thoughts and habits, we have to change our software. Consistency is a key factor in changing habits. Many people believe it takes 21 days to change a habit, but we don't necessarily agree. The stronger the software running the habit, the longer it may take to change.

> Let's say, for example, you've been eating one donut a day for the past six years. Your mind tells you that you've got to have a donut. Ignore that voice and think to yourself, I can replace that donut with a piece of fruit one day a week. The next week, try two days, and the next week, don't eat one for three days and so on. This process may take longer than 21 days, but remember that you've eaten your daily donut for almost six years straight. So rather then trying to quit cold turkey, work on replacing your unhealthy habit with a healthy one. By changing a habit gradually, eventually your mind and body adapt.

One of the primary reasons people don't work on changing negative habits is because it can be a slow process. Remember, though, each time you remove a bad habit, you replace it with a new and healthy habit that becomes ingrained in your subconscious. The old programming no longer serves you. How great would our lives be if we could replace unhealthy and unproductive habits with new, life-enriching ones?"[1] You are in charge of your thoughts, habits, and beliefs. Make a conscious decision to change the ones that set a bad example for your children. To change their results, change what you think about.

"Life happens, people get jaded, and things don't always go our way. We have to prepare our children for this by helping them to establish a positive belief system as well as giving them all the tools and elements in our own power to build them up before they enter the real world. Teach your children that they can do anything they want to do, that they can accomplish anything they want to accomplish. If you are able to instill that at an early age, they can move mountains. They can change the world. After all, what are our kids but our future?"[9]

ACTION STEPS

Refer to the Thought—Feeling—Result Cycle Image for this exercise.

1. Analyze a recent time you were angry and write down all of your thoughts that were going through your head at the time. Label how you felt and what was the outward way you expressed that feeling with your body? Then write down the action that you took and what was the result for you and your family members?

2. Repeat the same process as #1 with a time that you were experiencing happiness or joy.

3. What differences do you notice between your anger cycle versus your joy cycle?

For more writing space please visit
www.ParentOutLoud.com/STEP to download your free PlayBook.

CHAPTER 3

STAKING

*If we all did the things we are capable of,
we would astound ourselves.*

-Thomas Edison

"Mom, I don't understand. How do I just think something and make it happen in my head?" Meggie said. She was holding the invitation to be a bridesmaid for her best friend.

Cindy nodded toward the invitation, "Meggie, are you going to be at that wedding?

"Yes," she said emphatically.

"Do you have the money to fly to New York?"

"Not yet," she said.

"Do you know how you are going to get that money?" Cindy said.

"Well, no not yet."

"So how do you know you are going to New York?"

"I just am. I know I am going the be in that wedding!"

"Well, okay. There is your example. You know that some how; you're not sure specifically how, but you know that you are going to be a bridesmaid in that wedding and you're going to be able to pay for your ticket, your dress and your hotel, right?"

"Well of course!" she said.

"And all you did is think it. This is how it is for everything. You just have to decide."[6]

Focus—Where Are You Digging?

It's time to take a stand. Are you going to continue just living on autopilot with the programming your parents and community gave you or are you going to stake out a new path? Author Wilma Mankiller, stated that in Iroquois society, leaders are encouraged to remember **seven generations** in the past and consider **seven generations** in the future when making decisions that affect the people. Sometimes when we are just living day to day, it's easy to forget that many of the decisions we are making and lessons we are teaching our children will affect our family members that haven't yet been born.

When Cory and I focused on our limiting beliefs, we got a limited life. The biggest limiting belief for us was, "We can't afford it." The more we made this statement out loud, the more it seemed that we really didn't have enough money. We challenged that belief when we decided to invest in *ourselves* by studying with Bob

Proctor. We knew his program would teach us what we needed to make a massive change in our lives, yet weren't sure how we were going to pay for it. We decided to let go of our destructive thoughts and chose to believe that the money had to manifest somehow. We just stayed focused on "how can we do it?" Within 24 hours we were able to find funds in savings, stocks, unspent birthday and Christmas gift monies. We *could* afford it. We made a decision based on *what we wanted* rather than letting the price tag determine our decision.

One of our limiting beliefs regarding our kids was that we didn't want brilliant children because they would be too much work. We wanted average children who would go to school and fit in. Now we believe the complete opposite. Also, we used to think that if our kids weren't obedient, then we weren't good parents. But at the same time, we didn't want to be such strict parents that our children felt like they didn't have any personal power.

Take a moment and list any limiting beliefs in your life that may be preventing your children from reaching their potential.

Limiting Belief	Effect on Children
1. Smart students get straight A's.	**1.** You may have a B student doing their very best, yet feeling like a failure. This results in poor self-esteem.
2.	**2.**
3.	**3.**

For more writing space please visit
www.ParentOutLoud.com/STEP to download your free Play-Book.

If you don't believe you have any special gifts or talents and suffer from a low sense of self, how do you expect to teach your children to strive for success? Our children depend on us to set a good example for them, and if you live according to a constant stream of negative images and thoughts, you're passing those same destructive qualities on to them. We have to change our mental images to positive and abundant ones and teach them to do the same. When we find out that we're all here for a reason and what our strengths are, our kids do the same.[5]

The more we raise our awareness, the more freedom our children have to make their own choices and live their own lives. The subconscious mind is our command center, and each thought we allow to enter inevitably has an effect on our children. Any thought you expose yourself to repeatedly and impress upon the subconscious mind becomes fixed in this part of your personality. Do you ever tell yourself that you're stupid when you make a mistake? The same happens with your children. The more they hear and feel you think it, the easier this false belief transfers to them.

Focus on what you do want and you will attract that to you.

Our subconscious mind has *no choice* but to accept what we think. So we have to nourish it with healthy and encouraging thoughts.[5] There is a television show about what will happen when humans no longer inhabit the earth. This show is a good example of what can happen to structures abandoned and ignored. Sidewalks crack and break apart as the ground freezes and thaws. Vines and weeds take over buildings. Entire cities will be left in ruins by nature. If we don't make a conscious effort to take control of our self-destructive thoughts, they'll take over and crowd out the positive ones, leaving our life crumbled and in need of serious repair.

As you listed your limiting beliefs, think of how you can replace them with limit-less beliefs:

Limitless Beliefs	Effect on Children
1. My child has unique gifts that can't be measured by grades. They blossom and go after what they are passionate about.	**1.** They blossom and go after what they are passionate about.
2.	**2.**
3.	**3.**
4.	**4.**
5.	**5.**

For more writing space please visit
www.ParentOutLoud.com/STEP to download your free Play-Book.

Your subconscious mind is powerful, and when understood, improves not only your life but your children's lives as well. It expresses itself in your feelings, which lead to your actions and behavior. If you mistakenly focus on what you don't want, you will bring what you don't want into your life. The subconscious mind operates by Law in an orderly way. Your attitude is reflected in your self-image, which comes from your thoughts, feelings, and actions. So focus on what you do want and you will attract that to you. By learning to apply this knowledge to your life, you realize that you can give your family the power to have the best life possible.[5]

Ready for a Core Analysis?

Oftentimes, when a piece of property is cleared, the soil needs to be tested and analyzed for contamination. In the same way chemicals can leach through the soil into groundwater, your thoughts and emotions leach down through your beliefs, settle into your body's core, and become your constant feelings. Negative thoughts and beliefs are a toxic poison to your core, while positive thoughts are like compost resulting in massive growth and lush greenery in your life.

Now that you have a better understanding of how the mind and body work, it is much easier to shift your thought processes in both you and your kids. Who you are and what you become is a direct result of your beliefs. You are a reflection of those deeply embedded beliefs that have gradually, steadily, and consistently leached into your subconscious. Shifting from your current thoughts to those that you desire brings about transformation in your life. This is what is known as having a paradigm shift—adopting a new way of thinking, doing, and behaving.[5]

As parents, it's our responsibility to analyze our core beliefs and then help our children interpret and identify their experiences properly so that when something bad happens, they don't interpret it as, "Oh, I must be a horrible person." Just as a property surveyor places stakes to define the property lines, we need to give our children the tools to survey their experiences and translate them into a positive thought process. One of the best tools is language. Parents are an amazing resource to help children navigate the hurricane of emotions they feel. Part of developing emotional intelligence in our children is giving them a broad range of words for their feelings.

Over time, these positive remarks and sayings (see Key Paradigms at the end of the book) become habitual and help your children to succeed as adults. Help them to identify their emotions. Even if they've had a bad day or are just in a bad mood, encourage them to own their emotions. Let them use their words, and say, "Okay, my friend hurt my feelings. This how I feel right now, and I'm going to get over it and have a better day tomorrow." Teach them to leave their problems behind each night when they go to bed and that it isn't necessary to share with the world how miserable they feel. This is just victim mentality; successful people own up to their problems and transform them into opportunities.

Any thought embedded into the subconscious can be removed and replaced through repetition.

To replace limiting, self-defeating streams of thoughts, it is imperative to reduce the impact of these patterns. Be patient because this can take a good deal of time. Remember the donut example? Since it took a long time to acquire these beliefs, it may take time to replace them with new healthy beliefs. With all of this information about the subconscious mind, you may be thinking to yourself, "I will never be able to change my thought process." Yes, you can. Any thought embedded into the subconscious can be removed and replaced through repetition.[5]

A 30-day NASA experiment is an excellent example of repetition. In order to acclimate astronauts to the disorientation of space travel, they embarked on experimental training which involved wearing glasses that turned everything upside down. These glasses were to be worn day and night for 30 days. A totally unexpected phenomenon occurred. After day 30, the brain reprogrammed itself and flipped everything right side up again! There is one caveat however; you have to leave the glasses on for a consecutive 30 days. Those who removed them during the 30 days had to start all over again. The personal application of this powerful phenomenon is to realize the absolute necessity of repeating affirmations and focusing on visualizations consistently for a minimum of 30 days in order to capitalize on this life-changing practice. For maximum effect, you must practice reprogramming your subconscious for a consistent 30 days; no weekends off!

That sounds well and good, if you worked for NASA and were actually getting paid to participate in this study. But what if you're a busy parent like us who can barely get a shower some days? Just keep repeating your affirmations. You *will* feel it when they are having an effect. You will start to respond differently in situations, you'll feel better, and you'll be giving your children the freedom to live a life without limits. Isn't that more important?

We all want to be valued and appreciated. Instead of instilling much needed self-esteem and confidence into our children, at times we find it easier to criticize them. This habit is so automatic that we don't realize what we are saying. Words are powerful tools and have the ability to alter the course of a youngster's life. Stop and think about this for a moment. Do you still remember something your parents or an adult told you, which stays with you to this day?[5]

> *We all are inherently good and meant for greatness. It is just a matter of whether we choose to believe so.*

What we think about our children, whether we say it out loud or not, it is impressed upon them from a very young age. As parents, we are role models to our children; because they look up to us, we should constantly strive to build them up and make them realize that each of them is a winner in their own unique way. Leading by example is an absolutely critical component to parenting because they are watching us whether we know it or not. They observe the way in which we act when we're in public, when we communicate with others, and everything else that we do. What they see us do goes directly into their toolbox for future use.[5]

Our limiting beliefs can rob our children of their true insights about their gifts and purpose. Don't allow them to get stuck in a pattern of thoughts that are a barrier to their future progress. When you let the process of self-sabotage thinking choke out positive thoughts, you are allowing your children to accept less than they deserve.[5]

Part of developing emotional intelligence in our children is to give them a broad range of words for their feelings.

A couple of our children are very artistic. They are quick to criticize and condemn themselves for making mistakes in their paintings and drawings. We refuse to let them use negative language like, "I'm so stupid." Every time they say it, they knock a little chip out of their gift. Even so, it has taken several years for Justine to understand that repairing a mistake in her art often results in an opportunity for it to be better than she originally planned.

Don't continue to let negative thoughts take up space in your mind. Our limitations are self-imposed and can be overcome. Life presents many challenges. At times, these obstacles are more difficult for children to overcome than for adults. Most obstacles are small, but sometimes they are so big that they can stop a child from trying. After enough time, and continuous negative reinforcement, our children start to believe that their challenges are insurmountable.[5]

Fill your mind with positive and encouraging thoughts. Our results are a direct result of our thinking. Everything is controlled by our mind. If we want to change our life, we have to change our thinking. We've got to change what is going on inside our own mind and take responsibility for it. If you fill your mind with thoughts that contribute to positive behavior, your actions are proactive and therefore achieve successful results. Do your current results equal your potential? Keep in mind that your life is merely a reflection of your thoughts.[5]

As parents, we need to reinforce the positives in their lives. What do you think the outcome would be if you only told your children, "Believe in yourself," "Believe in your abilities," and "Believe that whatever the obstacle, you have the strength to overcome it"? All parents need to do is to teach their children to believe in themselves, and they will find a way to succeed. When our kids say, "I can't," we say "Oh, there is always a solution; how do you think you can solve this problem?" In response, our kids give us a solution that they see, and we then say, "I can see three more solutions," and then we give them our solutions. So now the problem that once seemed impossible has four solutions. Teaching your children to think this way expands their minds and gives them reasoning skills necessary for later in life. Our children are just as intelligent as we are. *They only lack the life experience.*

A strong belief in our abilities gives us the strength and the positive attitude that helps us find solutions to any obstacle and succeed at anything we put our minds to. If we believe in our abilities and ourselves, nothing can stop us. Believe that you will emerge successful. Believe that you are a winner. Believe that you deserve success. Are you beginning to see how important all of this is?

ACTION STEPS

1. Sit down with your children and write down any of their limiting beliefs.

2. Ask them, *"Is this absolutely true?"*

3. Write down three reasons that explain why the thought is false.

4. Talk about their feelings about the thought and what would happen if the thought disappeared.

5. Write an alternate belief that is 180 degrees opposite of the limiting belief. Talk about how much better their life would be if they can transform this limiting belief into a limitless belief.

6. The next time your child has a problem, make it into a game. See how many solutions you can find together.

7. Choose a limiting belief that you are going to spend the next 30 days changing.

For more writing space please visit
www.ParentOutLoud.com/STEP to download your free PlayBook.

CHAPTER 4

THE DRAWING BOARD

*Success in life is becoming what you
truly want to be.*

-Wallace D. Wattles

"I am writing a book, just like you Mimi! I have a book idea."

"You do?" Natalie absolutely adored her grandson's creativity.

"I already have my cover," he said proudly.

Natalie glanced over at her daughter Hope and smiled. Then she looked back at Ian and inhaled deeply with joy.

"Really? Bring it out. Let's see it, Ian!"

He marched over to her with his copy. "This is my cover, Mimi." He placed his list of possible book titles and the cover in her lap.

Natalie beamed as she looks over his concept. He had put his favorite Tony Hawke t-shirt on the copy machine and pushed the print button.

She laughed. "We might have some copyright infringement situations here but I love that you are thinking Ian! Most 10- and 11-year-olds aren't thinking about book titles, book covers, or finding more ways to increase their value. You are a very special boy and a gift to this world."[26]

Sharpen Your Pencil

As you learned in Chapter Three, you may have to dig around a bit in your mind to unearth some destructive thought processes. Do you believe people have a genetic propensity for success? Are they born with an innate ability to accomplish great feats? To this we must answer an emphatic "No!" Each one of us is capable of creating success. Take a look at Oprah Winfrey, Bill Gates, or Richard Branson. They are no different than any of us. We're all born on a level playing field.

In our studies with personal development giant Bob Proctor, we've learned many of the underlying principles of success, and one of the first is raising your awareness. Think of your awareness being like the circular ripples in the water when you throw a rock. When you grow, your awareness expands to the next ripple. It can only go one direction—out. Once you expand your awareness, you can't go back toward the rock. The more you grow in self-awareness, the better you understand your feelings and why you behave in certain ways. This, in turn, makes you aware of the effects your behaviors have on your children.

Our parents' toolkit is outdated. We need an upgrade. How many times have you caught yourself saying or thinking, "Oh my gosh! I hated it when my mom said this to me when I was a kid.

I swore I would never say it, but I just did." We have to decide to change those beliefs. We need a parenting upgrade; doing so automatically equips our children to live in their future, not our past. It's our responsibility to our children, to ourselves, to our neighbors, and to our society that we continue to do the work that makes us better people. Learning shouldn't end after High School or College; the classroom just looks different.

> *Not only can you have the life you've always dreamed of but you can give your children the tools to build the life of their dreams as well.*

We are given the opportunity and knowledge to change and create the lives we want for both our family and ourselves. If we want to improve the results in our children's lives, we not only have to change our thoughts, we also have to increase our level of awareness. By this, we mean that you must take a look at your life through a different lens. How do you act in certain situations? Do your children mimic those reactions? Are you meant for more than just an ordinary existence? Does your enthusiasm and zest for life encourage your children to follow their dreams as well?

Along with upgrading our parenting skills, we need to teach our children to look at more events through an empowered viewpoint, and less through the eyes of repetitively instilled, limiting beliefs. Once we become aware of our destructive thoughts, we can then make a conscious decision to change them. Rather than live in a world based on other's opinions, why not delve into a deeper understanding of who

If we want to improve the results in our children's lives, we not only have to change our thoughts, we also have to increase our Level of Awareness.

we truly are? With an increased state of awareness, we're able to dig into our true purpose in life, which is important if we're going to live according to God's will, rather than society's.[5] This, in turn, enables us to grow as well as give our children the tools necessary to succeed in life.

There are seven Levels of Awareness. In order to improve your success and help your children to reach their full potential, we need to progress through these Levels of Awareness and strive to live at the highest state. The level at which you live directly influences the quality of both your child's life and yours. While reading the following descriptions, determine where you are today. Is this where you want to be, or would you like to aspire to be more?[5]

SEVEN LEVELS OF AWARENESS

Survival

This is the lowest level of awareness. It is our instinctive level and only allows us to live according to a series of stimulus responses. Many of you may know this as fight or flight. Little, if any, thought is used at this level because your actions are based on instincts and you are relying on your physical senses. A baby's actions are good examples of this. They cry when their diapers are wet or when they are hungry. Their actions are reactionary.[5]

As parents, however, if we live in a reactionary state and yell and scream every time something doesn't go our way, we're setting an example for our children that adult temper tantrums and flying off the handle at the slightest provocation is appropriate behavior. Our primary focus needs to be how to help our children make choices that reflect who they are rather than choices based on emotion or reactions. We need to teach them to view a situation in terms of what they can control and what part of the situation is out of their control.

As we grow and mature, it is important to realize that there are going to be obstacles in our lives. Not learning how to step back and look for the positives in these types of situations will have a prolonged effect on our children's well being. Let's take the scenario that your daughter comes home one day from school and is upset because she received an F on her history test. Instantly, you grab your keys, jump in the car, and race to the school to demand an explanation from her teacher. Your reaction was an automatic interpretation that happened instantaneously, without your having thought about it. What type of an example did you just set for your daughter? If you don't get what you want, blame someone else? Success doesn't require any work on her behalf? Rather than jumping to conclusions, why not take the time and ask her if she studied? Or ask her what she learned from the situation and how she can do better next time? Sit down together to discuss whether or not there are any different ways to prepare for the next exam. We all have the parental instinct to protect our children, and we certainly don't want to see them upset, but we have to remember that they mimic our actions. So the next time you feel yourself starting to react to a situation, stop for a moment; think about the ramifications of your actions before letting your basic survival instincts take control.

Mass

This awareness level is where the majority of people live their lives. At this level, we spend much of our time concerned about what others think about us. Common questions at this level include,

"What will my coworkers think?" "What will my parents think?" The problem with this is that you don't actually know what others think of you. Their opinions may be entirely different than what you believe them to be. We can't live based on our assumptions of what other people think. We have no control over what others think, and it is none of their business anyway. One of our favorite quotes is, "Great people talk about *ideas*. Average people talk about *things*. Small people talk about other *people*." Those who have the courage to stand apart from the crowd and let their ideas flourish are the ones who lead the most fulfilling lives. What do you spend most of your time talking about—ideas, things, or people?[5]

When we operate at the Mass Level, we conform to what we believe everyone else thinks about us and we tend to follow the crowd. It is important to understand that we are each born into this world as unique individuals, but our society really doesn't encourage individuality. We are encouraged to dress alike, talk alike, follow the rules, get a job, get a house, start a family, and so forth. We are raised into conformity. Peer pressure pushes children into living this way. If you don't dress a certain way, you won't have any friends. If you don't smoke, you won't be cool. One of the biggest fears of a child is isolation, which is why so many follow along blindly. This fear of isolation filters over into their adulthood in the form of settling for a job we don't like or accepting an unhealthy relationship just to keep from being lonely.[5]

Great people talk about ideas. Average people talk about things. Small people talk about other people.

We recently took a family vacation, and on the way home, we passed a train covered with gang graffiti. As the spray-painted cars rolled along the tracks, we couldn't help but notice the amount of talent it must have taken to paint such detailed letters. How different would the lives of those gang members be if their gift was nurtured and they were encouraged to follow their dreams? Instead, they found comfort in the acceptance of their peers. The moment you become aware of the value of your uniqueness, you give the world a gift. If you let others decide your future, you'll live their ideas and dreams, not your own. Popularity should never be a guide on how to live.

Aspiration

If you were to ask yourself, "What do I want for my child?" one of your answers would be that they be happy. One of the main ways to find fulfillment is to learn about all that life has to offer. Our children are going to learn from us. If for no other reason than the love we have for our children, we need to teach them that life is about learning. It is a journey and we don't stop developing after we are out of school. In this Level of Awareness, we realize that there is something more to life, but we don't move any further than that realization. We like to call these types of people eternal dreamers. In school, we were taught not to daydream. How many times did you ever stare out the window during class, imagining flying to the moon or donning a cape and saving the world, only to hear your teacher say, "Stop daydreaming and pay attention?" Dreams are wonderful preludes to what the future holds. There is one caveat however; you must take deliberate action for those dreams to ever be transformed into reality.[5]

If you dream about inventing a car that runs on water and then do nothing to prepare the way for that dream to come to fruition, then that so-called dream is useless. You will go to your grave with that dream inside of you. However, if you hold thoughts of unlimited possibilities and then take the appropriate actions toward reaching those possibilities, you are heading toward those dreams. What's even more exciting is that those dreams are headed toward you. They will come true.[5]

> Albert Einstein's story is especially compelling in relation to dreams. Einstein did his best thinking while daydreaming. Did you know that his professors dismissed him as a boy who wasted his time daydreaming? As an adult, he was unable to find permanent employment in Germany; he worked for several years as a clerk in the Swiss Patent Office that allowed him the freedom to spend several hours a day staring out of the window in contemplation. Because he held thoughts of endless possibilities and he continued to daydream, Einstein was able to pursue his goal of understanding the underlying unity that governs reality and eventually give the world the Theory of Relativity.

Individual

After aspiring to be something better, some people begin to acknowledge that they are worthwhile, unique individuals capable of amazing achievements. But as we mentioned earlier, in order for you to reach your goals you have to take action, which leads us to the fourth Level of Awareness—Individual. In this level, we start to express our uniqueness. Remember there is no one else like you in this world, and you were put here for a purpose. In chapter two, we discussed the conscious and subconscious mind and this level is where you begin to use your conscious mind, your thinking mind. Here is where you begin to question the present. "Is this all there is?" This is where you start wondering what you want in your life. "What would happen if ...?" Living your life on autopilot, just going through the motions doesn't give you the ability to help your children decide what their purpose is, either.[5]

"How many times have you wanted something better or different so your life can be great? Is there a little voice inside saying, 'You can do better!' When children start to search for a greater meaning in life, they are less apt to focus on what is happening around them; instead, they focus on what is happening inside them. The moment you realize that you are unique, that your original thoughts and contributions are essential to this world, is the moment that you begin to achieve great things.

Children have to wake up to the truth of who they are within. The desire to be something better and greater than what they are in this moment, has to build to the intensity of a raging fire. In order to be more, to do more, and to have more, the discomfort within has to get incredibly uncomfortable. A child has to get so bored that they get sick of watching TV when they get home or they get fed up with being so tired from just going to school, coming home and going to bed.

Until you reach that point where we start to look for other answers, there is nothing that you can do for yourself or your children. You're too comfortable, and change is uncomfortable. You will be drawn to others who just seem different, wondering, 'What have you got? You are different. What makes you so different from me?'"[30]

Our friend Deena Morton has a saying: "There is a diamond inside of everybody that is in rough form." She's right. You were born perfect. You are the most precious, perfect stone ever, but life and other people's perception and their beliefs start to tarnish it, and soon you've lost your sparkle. It is easy to take on other people's habits, perceptions of the world, and their negative beliefs. As a child transitions into an adult, it's important they ignore what others are doing, saying, and thinking to keep their diamond from being tarnished. We can teach our children to let their diamond sparkle early on and continue into adulthood so that the world will see how amazing they are, what gifts God gave them, and to live into their potential. Wouldn't that be a great gift to give to your children? But how can you, if you haven't done it for yourself?

Discipline

This level is absolutely critical to the person who has aspired to break away from the Mass Level of Awareness. We concentrate on the ability to focus on our goals despite distractions and outside influences. This is similar to the gravitational force of the earth. With such a large mass, the earth has a strong gravitational force that keeps items on its surface. For a rocket to break away from the gravitational force of the earth, it has to have tremendous thrust. That thrust is similar to the discipline needed for us to walk away from other's opinions and our own paradigms in order to follow through with our own aspirations. To become better parents, we have to continue to grow and move forward in life.[5]

> "When we drive with our children, we listen to motivational CDs as well as read them books that are relevant to adults, like Napoleon Hill's Think and Grow Rich. They get excited when they hear ideas that help them. These enriching opportunities enable us to teach and stretch their minds. We constantly watch, listen, and absorb ideas that give them the tools to succeed. We dialog with our children all of the time."[17]

When parents look for personal growth books, it requires an investment of time. Since time management is important for all of us, we must gauge our time carefully. Just as we did with the Stickman picture of the mind for our daughter, we rephrase some of the items in the books so our children more easily understand them.

Experience

"Actress Bette Davis once said, 'In order for you to be a good parent, you've got to make it okay that at sometime in the parenting process, your children are going to hate your guts.' This statement is true because we live in a society in the world where we value what people think of us, particularly our children. There are so many parents who want to be their child's friend. There has to be a distinct separation between parenting and friendship. Liking you and respecting you are entirely different. Be prepared to go through several periods of time when you suggest ideas to your kids, and they aren't going to have a clue about what you're saying."[22] Realize, though, that as they grow in their Level of Awareness, they will start to understand what you're telling them.

As you apply discipline in your life, you will soon elevate to a new Level of Awareness, Experience. The experience you gain reinforces your awareness of your own abilities. Regarding your children's lives, there is no substitute for experience. Teach them to get involved with causes that are important to them and take action. Find some charitable causes in your area. Volunteer to help feed the homeless on Thanksgiving or start a community beautification project. Experience helps us improve our overall awareness. As we experience life, we see new opportunities that had been previously hidden. This is what expanding your awareness is all about. When you learn and experience something new, your circle of awareness has just gotten bigger. Learning to apply experience sets you apart and takes you further in your quest for a life of fulfillment.[5]

There is a substantial difference between learning and experience. Learning is often based in theory, while experience is through real-world applications.

Let's say, for example, you decide to coach your son's soccer team. You played the sport in high school and college and know what it takes to be successful. Another coach in the league, however, hasn't ever played but has read several different books on the subject. Which one do you think is more equipped to handle the job? Hint: it's not the one who read the books.

Fortunately or unfortunately, our past experiences have shaped who we are.[5] In the case of the soccer coach, those past experiences will help the person be a better coach to his or her child. However, we may have past experiences in our lives, which we may not even be aware of, that shape our current actions. In some cases, our experiences may give us results that we do not want. We need to make a conscious effort to create new experiences in order to replace those of the past; which allows us to make a shift within us toward the new way of life that we want.

Mastery

When we reach the Mastery Level of Awareness, we utilize a higher level of thought, and we respond to situations instead of reacting to them. Along with this comes a higher level of imagination, creativity, enthusiasm, excitement, and gratitude. Our habits no longer control us, and we rid ourselves of any limiting beliefs. It is through mastery of your mind that you are able to reach the pinnacle of life. We help our kids physically as well as mentally to understand they have control over how they feel. If, for example, they cry, we talk to them and try to comfort them by saying, "Well, do you like the way you are feeling right now?" By just teaching them that they are in control of their emotions, they can change their energy.[5]

When you finally overcome your fears and anxiety, you quickly begin to see signs of progress toward your goals. Your subconscious mind will not be filled with doubt but with optimism and unlimited possibilities. Once we reach the mastery Level of Awareness, we know that we are on a one-way journey to success in everything we put our minds to and the world is ours for the taking.[5]

Where do you fall on the scale of awareness? How about your children? To achieve the Mastery Level, you have to examine yourself and your lifestyle with an open and honest mind. We found that we couldn't move to this level without help and guidance from other mentors and teachers who daily live in the Mastery Level of Awareness. Don't judge yourself or your actions too harshly. Just pay attention and become aware of your feelings, behaviors, words, and thoughts, especially around your children. As you become more aware of your actions, you move up the Levels toward Mastery. You understand you need to change the words you use when talking with your children. In doing this, you teach them valuable life lessons, and most importantly, you help mold the thoughts they hold in their minds. True self-awareness is a crucial step to living a fulfilled life. Move toward mastery of your awareness. This gives your children a huge head start over others, and with their mastery, they will live a life of abundance.

As you become more aware of your actions, you will begin to move up the Levels toward Mastery.

Interior Floor Plan—Our True Self

We've spoken quite a bit about dreams in this chapter. Dreams expand the boundaries of our inner self. Unfortunately, far too many of us aren't following our dreams. Once upon a time, a long time ago, each one of us had a dream. Maybe it was to be a professional singer, a writer, or maybe something as simple as traveling to exotic destinations. Ask any second grader what they want to be when they grow up and you'll hear every answer from president to doctor to astronaut. But then life happens. You get married, have kids, find a job, and just get busy with the everyday happenings and forget you even had a dream. Worse yet, maybe you just dismissed your dream altogether, thinking that it could never happen for you now. Over the years, you've slowly let your walls close in around you; suddenly, your true self is confined to a small 700 square foot apartment with no way out.[5]

Throughout our lives, our identity has been strongly influenced by society. From our childhood, we learn what is "right" and "wrong," what we "should" and "shouldn't" do, what is "true" and what "cannot be true." We learn that, if we want to be worthy, we have to attend college and find a well paying job to support our family. Also, as we grew up, we watched our parents go to the same job day after day for thirty five to forty years just so they could retire but not have the energy to do the things they wanted to do. We have a friend whose mother taught school for twenty-plus years and was miserable every minute of it. When asked why she stayed, she said she was lucky to have a job. Who wants to live in a world where you have to stick with a job you hate and then feel lucky to have that job? We should make rational decisions, right? Why do we settle for any job that we can get? Our careers don't define who we are, and we cannot let them have the power to keep us from what we truly desire.[5]

Is there anyone in this world whose last wish would be to spend more time at work? Of course not. (Okay, quick sidebar: yes, there are some of you out there who truly love your work, but you are the minority.) Our real desire is to do what invigorates and energizes us. What is truly important to us, to our deeper, true self, comes from the answers to "What have I done that I will be proud of at the end of my life? What will leave a legacy to my children?" The events in life that we remember most and we are most proud of are what define our identity. Many of us live in disharmony with our true desires. Unfortunately, society imposes more pressure on our social self than we can comfortably handle.[5]

Ruler or Pretender?

"What kind of teaching are parents doing for their children if they haven't gone through this process of growth and increased awareness themselves? We are always interested in the idea of helping kids express themselves and using that to enhance their social and emotional development. This becomes especially important during middle-school ages. This is the time developmentally that they are supposed to be engaged in figuring out who they are. If we aren't guiding our 'tweens and teens to find their passions, they end up trying to please someone else by being their clone. If your children feel pressure to fit in with the kids at school even though they know that they aren't good peers, they may succumb to that pressure and not feel good about it. These new relationships can create problems and cause your children to do something they'll regret.

What society says doesn't matter. You are the ruler of your life.

If our children spend too many years acting like someone else, they soon forget that they are pretending. They end up graduating from high school or entering college having missed years of opportunities to discover who they really are and practice navigating through the world as their true selves. Then they move into the adult world still not knowing who they are or what their special gifts are. Suddenly, they are 40 and they are parents. What kind of teaching will they do? How can they guide their magnificent children into adulthood? This is why personal development is so critical. If you put it on the back burner too long, you'll make immature, poor choices, and you'll miss the juice of life."[4]

The people around us are constantly trying to persuade us one way or the other. What we have to realize is that what society says doesn't matter. You are the ruler of your life. Just because your career is going well, your bank account is fat, and everyone believes you to be a success, doesn't mean it is true in your eyes. Earl Nightingale, a pioneer in the field of personal development, said that people are successful if they are pursuing a worthy goal or ideal. Therefore, no matter what society says, you are successful if you are pursuing something that is worthwhile in your own eyes. All that really matters is how you feel about where you are taking your life.[5]

Paying attention to our feelings in order to understand what really matters to us is often an alien concept. It is, however, our feelings that we must explore in order to find our true selves. When we take a good, honest look at what we feel, we get a glimpse at what we are truly meant to be. Our logical self has buried this other part of our identity. In order to tap into, and free the side of us that is the true reflection of who we are, we must connect with the emotions that we experienced during times of sincere happiness, pure joy, and elation. You can have a life of genuine happiness. You just have to identify what you love to do, form a basic plan to create that end, and begin nailing the pieces into place.[5]

It is your purpose that keeps you going and striving for your goals despite the obstacles that may come in the way.

Interior Elevations

All good construction projects start with a blueprint. If we don't have a good schematic of a building or house, the end result may be something entirely different from what we planned for in the beginning. Our lives are the same. How can we build upon a foundation if we don't have a master plan? What type of foundation are we constructing for our children? The ancient Greek philosopher Plato said "It is enlightenment to know oneself." We are lucky enough to know our purpose in life. Most people don't, and that is a shame. We encourage everyone to discover that purpose within you because it drives you to the next level. It is your purpose that keeps you going and striving for your goals despite the obstacles that may come along the way; and they will come along. That is part of life.

> Your past and your possessions do not define you.
> Let go and move forward with a realistic,
> confident belief in yourself.

"You can't experience the richness, the wonders, the glory, and the heights of success without feeling the valley of pain and even depression or the worries at the bottom. A lot of people don't understand that. They want everything to be happy all the time. How can you know what happiness is if you never experience sadness? It is the acceptance and understanding of that concept that allows us to grow even further."[9] Live in the now and do what you're truly passionate about. Children have to be guided based on who they are inside. A lot of that is predetermined. It is like a mystery, and it is exciting as it starts to unfold. We tell our kids, "We love you all equally but do not treat you all the same, because you are so different."

What we need to do for one child is different from what we need to do for another. You must not let your belief about yourself be biased by anyone else. The opinions of others such as your parents, spouse, coworkers, or friends don't matter.[5] For example, your parents may have told you that you weren't competent or good enough. Perhaps that has played out in your life as an unsatisfactory job, a frustrating family life, and a personal life devoid of elated highs. It doesn't have to be that way. You have the power within yourself to be the competent person that we all have inside. Don't let the beliefs of others define who you are. Make a mental shift and decide to take control of who you are.

Why are you here on this planet? What gifts have you been given that you can give back to the world?

Your past doesn't define you.[5] Mistakes, relationships, and your previous actions are merely a collection of experiences in your memory. You are not your job, car, home, or financial portfolio. These are just possessions that can come and go. Once you understand that your past and your possessions are only external labels, which hold no security, you can move forward with a realistic, confident belief in yourself. Your security is within you. No matter who rejects you, no matter how many times you "fail," you are still you. Those rejections and failures are just experiences. You learn from experience.

> As the two of us traveled through life, several questions surfaced, things like," Why am I here?" "What is my purpose?" "What makes me get out of bed in the morning and live my life each day?"

Why are you here on this planet? What gifts have you been given that you can give back to the world? For some people, this understanding of their purpose emerges relatively early in their journey. For others, knowledge of their purpose eludes them for quite a long time. Whether the answer arrives quickly or takes months, we realize that we can only be happy when we pursue our purpose. Information from the academic fields of science, education, philosophy, and medicine are coming around to the same point. They all speak of the benefits of self-care. To borrow from the airline industry; You've got to put the oxygen mask on yourself first. What our grandmothers always said couldn't be truer: "You can't love anyone until you love yourself." If you are working on self-love, you are going to be as effective a parent as possible, and all of your relationships will improve.

> *Visualize your dream, define it, and then go for it!*
> *Choose to be happy and share that*
> *happiness with the world.*

Drafting Your Plans

We are not taught to figure out why we are on this planet and state it in two or three sentences. It is important to take the time to look inside of ourselves and find the plan for our lives inherent in our purpose. Then we are able to feel successful and happy with our lives as we live out our purpose. Purpose gives us meaning and hope beyond our present circumstances. Although you may believe that you or your life doesn't have much meaning, you actually do have value to offer. You were not put here by mistake, and you aren't just taking up space on this planet.[5] As motivational speaker Les Brown says, "You survived out of 40 million sperm. If you beat those odds, you can win at anything!" If you feel as though your life lacks purpose, meaning, or is just missing that certain "something," you need to listen your inner voice. The manifestation of your purpose is as unique and precious as you are.

There is nothing more influential to your children than for them to see you passionately engaged in something you love. We truly believe that if everyone in this world stopped to figure out what they wanted to do and loved to do, this world would be a magnificent place. "There is a way for you to do what you love right where you are, wherever you are, in your life right now. Your children benefit because you are a happier person and a happier parent. You have more fun with your children when you are with them. You are not resentful, feeling, 'Oh, I am just biding my time until these guys go to college, and then I can start picking up my life from where it was.' This is one of the things that has been really so incredible to learn while studying about ourselves. Personal growth and self-development is just the study of the self. You don't have to wait until the kids are all grown up. You can do it right now!

Now is an even better time to do it than when your children are all grown because if you put your life on hold, you are wasting part of your life, not only for yourself, but also for your children. You are not able to give to them the abundance that you would be able to give them if you were living a passionate life pursuing something that you truly love."[19]

Filling In the Details

Each of us has a divine blueprint. We embody our purpose in many different ways. For example, we may be attracted to certain people and situations and relate to our environment in our own unique fashion. Some may love acting as a caregiver to small children or the elderly; others may wish to spend their time teaching. You may even enjoy drawing and painting, or singing and dancing, while your spouse may read voraciously or tinker with their computer. All the natural tendencies within, if allowed to flourish and expand, lead you to manifesting your purpose, and give you joy along the way.[5]

So, let us ask you this one question. If all of your expenses were covered, how would you fill your days? Would you travel, become a photographer or artist, volunteer in a third-world country, or do something else? Whatever your answer is, that is what you are meant to do. We have yet to meet someone who says, "I want to be the best TV viewer in the world." Yet by our actions, many of us slowly attain that title. We are either moving forward, or we are moving backwards, which is why is so important that we continue to grow and learn and teach our children to do the same.

As you find your purpose, your passions start to come alive, you start to believe in yourself more, and you do something that builds your self-confidence. When your self-confidence steps up a little bit, you try something else, you believe a little bit more, your self-confidence comes up a little bit more, and your children sense the change in you. Make the decision to be more consciously aware of how and what you are thinking, and then start asking yourself better questions. That is what makes you feel alive.[5] We participate in several MasterMind calls as part of our personal growth. This is when a group of like-minded people get together to brainstorm ideas to improve each others lives and businesses. One day, Justine said, "When am I going to have a MasterMind call?" Once your children see you actively pursue your passions in life, it ignites in them a desire to do the same.

Do you know what your children really want?

Through the journey of finding your purpose, as well as realizing that only you are responsible for your life, you become unattached to specific outcomes or to the thoughts and feelings of others. When you act from this place of clarity and confidence, you influence others. You don't have to get them to do anything. When you act selfishly to get what you want, you meet resistance. When you clearly desire a certain outcome, and you are not stressed about when it will manifest itself because you know it will at the right time, you are living in a powerful position. Finding and following your purpose gives you a voice of confidence and the ability to fulfill what you were put on this earth to do.[5] Living according to your purpose is essential, not only for you but for the good of everyone, especially your children. As they see you moving through life confidently, they will, in turn, move through their lives with confidence.

Success is something we can learn, master, and teach our children. When you're in alignment with your passion in life, the whole world tends to move forward effortlessly. Doors open automatically. People seem to appear on your path who can help you get what you want. You're often in the right place at the right time. Life just seems to flow without any resistance. Once we are in alignment, then we are open to life's possibilities and opportunities. The more you are in alignment with your life purpose, the less life seems to be a struggle in other areas as well. What have you always been dreaming about? Do you see your children with dreams of their own? Our dream in writing this book is to help you increase your and your children's Level of Awareness, help you and your children find the reason why you are here on earth, and help you teach your children to realize their potential so they can manifest their personal dreams. As the late "Golden Rule" Jones, former mayor of Toledo, Ohio, said, "What I want for myself, I want for everyone." Do you know what your children really want?[5]

ACTION STEPS

Map out the blueprint for your life. Write down your own personal purpose statement. It should be short, concise and contain only two to three sentences. Here's an example of our purpose statements:

Anamarie's Purpose

(1) Through writing, art, and teaching, I enrich and inspire (2) my children and the world's children ages 1 to 101, to (3) understand and experience the Laws of the Universe and the teachings of Bob Proctor. (4) The products of my creativity will cause immeasurable joy and progressive impact, be in harmony with the Law of Compensation, and will improve the quality of life for my family, community, country, and the world.

Cory's Purpose

(1) Through my writing, programs, and modeling with the raising of my own children, (4) I will help improve the quality of life for (2) families around the world (3) by helping them raise healthy children who have the belief that they have the power to do and achieve all that they desire.

Now use the following page to create your personal purpose statement and Vision Statement.

Four parts of a Purpose Statement:

1. Essential Action—How do you engage in the world: teaching, writing, coaching, building, creating, etc.?

2. The Beneficiary—Who is influenced by your actions?

3. Central Concern—What your action is creating?

4. Intended Impact—What will happen?

_____

_____

_____

_____

Vision Statement

This is where you define a little more how you are going to go about executing your purpose—writing, coaching, opening businesses, investing in real estate, etc. This should be very detailed, like describing a movie. Take your time with this portion. It may take several days or weeks to develop and expand.

There are two parts:

1. Why—Why do you think something is your purpose? How does it make you feel?

2. What—A description of your ideal life living on purpose. You are wearing what, living where, driving what, expressing your gifts and talents how; describe your work, your customers, the impact of each day, your travel, etc. Use rich color and description. Use as many pages as you need.

For more writing space please visit
www.ParentOutLoud.com/STEP to download your free PlayBook.

CHAPTER 5

LAYING THE FOUNDATION

*Luck is what happens when preparation
meets opportunity.*

–Seneca (Roman philosopher, mid-1st century AD)

"Mom, can I share my Lego™ wish list with you?"

Lisa paused from cleaning the dishes to listen to her eight-year-old son. He really wanted several of the expensive, specialized block sets. They had parrots and pirates, and knights in shining armor. Lisa had grown up with the simple sets of blocks and wheels in the 1970s, which she had passed on to her children. Although she sympathized with his desire to have better Lego™ building blocks, with five children to feed, she couldn't justify the expense.

"Okay Abe, look. Everything in our life, in our physical world began with an idea. It began as a thought. If you want these big sets, what you need to do is this; I want you to write it down on paper. We are going to stick it on the fridge. You just picture yourself having it. Imagine how it's going to feel. Allow yourself to plant the seed in your mind. Everything begins with a seed. It's not up to us to know how it's going to happen, but it is up to us to plant the seed and visualize it and feel as though it is real."

Abe started getting excited. "Okay. I can do that."

"Then get to work. See what you can do to maybe earn the money that would pay for them or just start moving your feet."

Part of Lisa doubted that she could teach him this principle. What if it didn't work for him? Her fear was getting in the way, but she kept it to herself. Consciously, she knew her fears were ridiculous because this works no matter what. Abe and Lisa didn't have a clue how the bricks would arrive, but she had convinced him that this process works. The younger the children are, the less scrutiny they put on something like this. Their advantage is that they just don't know that it might not work.

Lisa got to work also. She and her husband started searching online auctions for a really good deal, but they were not having any luck. One day while her husband was at work, a coworker came up to him.

"You know what? My son has outgrown his toy building bricks. Do you have anyone in your family who would like some?"

His eyes grew huge in disbelief. "Yeah! What have you got?"

"We have all kinds of sets, including the booklets and manuals. I've got some family members who might have more. Let me get back with you."

By the time she talked to all of her family members who also had outgrown brick play, they pulled together a big chest full of blocks. It was about four feet wide, three feet deep, and about four feet tall, full of more than $1,000 worth of mint-condition bricks.

Lisa and Tom went home and divided the thousands of building bricks into four big boxes, wrapped them, and put them under the Christmas tree. Abe's face revealed his utter shock when he opened the first box. There were the pirates, parrots, and alligators, the sails and the ladders; everything was visualizing. His eyes were huge. He was so excited. Then he opened the second box; the same reaction. By the third box he fell to the floor. He was flat on the floor with amazement—and there was still the fourth box.

It just showed Abe, and it showed his parents, that the Law of Perpetual Transmutation works every time. They have done it with so many different things, including increasing their income. It's been a decade since Lisa started seeing this really work. Even now, every time it happens, she is still just as amazed but no longer surprised.[23]

Design Rules

Every construction project needs a solid foundation. It is important to take great care in properly setting up the foundation because the success of the project, whether it is a large house or small tool shed, relies heavily on the care and effort that has been put into the site preparation. Just as concrete provides a strong and stable foundation for our buildings, the Universal Laws of Nature anchor a family. One important factor we need to realize regarding these Laws is that for everything to function properly, there has to be structure. Without structure, our world or Universe, in fact, would be in utter chaos. By incorporating the Universal Laws of Nature into our lives, we will not only find ourselves living in harmony with those Laws, but our lives will also be tuned to the Universe in such a way that we will have fulfilling, abundant lives filled with joy, peace, happiness, and good health.[5]

Perhaps you have heard of one of the Laws; the Law of Attraction, since it was the featured topic of the movie, *The Secret*, but that is just the tip of the iceberg. These Laws are the unwavering and unchanging principles that rule our entire Universe and are the means by which it continues to thrive and exist. How many people do you know who seem to have it all? You may be wondering what their secret is. We can tell you what it is without even meeting them. They are taking actions that are in harmony with the powerful Universal Laws. It does not matter whether they are aware of or even understand these Laws. The Universal Laws of Nature are working at all times, in all places.[5]

> **If we want to improve the results in our children's lives, we not only have to change our thoughts, we also have to increase our Level of Awareness.**

Unfortunately, most parents either aren't aware of these Laws or don't take the time or put forth the effort to develop an awareness of how to align their parenting with these Laws. However, if parents passed on the awareness of these Laws they would, with exact certainty, give their children the tools to live a prosperous life. Instead, most parents try to give their children happiness through spending more money on them and giving them more material possessions.[5] Several of the parents we interviewed for this book raise their children according to these Laws. They understand the Universal Laws and apply them daily.

Level Ground?

Developing an understanding of and learning to align with these Laws leads your family down a path filled with hope, abundance, happiness, joy, fulfillment, and peace. Some people don't abide by these Laws because they aren't aware of them. If we were to ask you if you understood the Law of Gravity, you might say yes or you might say no. Either way, this Law would still govern you. Your children become aware of this Law if they fall off of their bicycle or out of a tree. Everyone, no matter their level of awareness of gravity, would fall to the ground and be killed if they stepped off the top of a skyscraper. ... Or would they? Everyone who is aware of the Law of Gravity could align themselves and work with the Law. They could use a parachute to safely land after departing from the top of the skyscraper.

Albert Einstein believed that the Universe operates according to a structured set of Laws. History indicates that, along with Einstein, many of the great scientists were raised in an environment that taught them in thousands of ways that there are Natural Laws in the Universe and that those Laws are to be respected. Once we learned of these Laws, they opened our eyes to the fact that the Universe is orderly. Passing this knowledge on to our children is one of the most important goals and outcomes of our successful parenting. Before we can fully understand these Laws, however, we must know who created the Universe. In school, some of us were taught about the Big Bang Theory, which theorizes that a great explosion created the Universe. But who created the explosion? The gigantic mass of material didn't just appear. It had to be created by someone or something.

There is one truth that all people share to some degree or another. That is, there is a higher power that controls the Universe and what we get out of it. No matter what your religious beliefs are, this higher power is the one who created the Universe and gives us everything we need. For some, this is God; for others, this is an Infinite Being. Regardless of what we call Him/Her, everything in the Universe is created in its image and likeness. This is why the Universe is so powerful. Certain Laws had to be created for it to operate in harmony. Many people argue that these Laws are made up or are those of man. If you study the Bible, you'll easily be able to find them. In the back of the book we've included various sections of the Bible where you can find passages related to the Natural Laws of the Universe for further study.[5]

Parents who teach their children the Natural Laws of the Universe prepare them for success. "It is tremendously valuable to verbally say which Law is actually happening for your child; like the Law of Vibration. If you teach them the term for what they experience or what they identify, down the road it can be just, 'Hey, sweetie … Vibration.' The whole conversation is completed with just one word."[23] We'll talk more about the Law of Vibration later in this chapter.

A Concrete Footing

A firm understanding of these Laws is a distinguishing factor between reaching your dreams by accomplishing your goals and living a life of mediocrity. Just as the concrete footing is the base support for the walls of a home, when young people discover that there is an order to the Universe and certain Laws govern it, this supports them in realizing that they can then use this knowledge to master any area of life they want.[5] The fundamental Laws enable our children to meet the challenges of life with confidence. When we started teaching our children about the Laws, we noticed a positive change in their behavior. Several things just started to make sense to them.

These Universal Laws govern every aspect of existence and are responsible for determining your life experience. Just like the Law of Gravity, these Laws operate with precise, predictable, and unwavering certainty and make no distinctions or judgments in how they operate or whom they work for. They are at work 100 percent of the time, regardless of your awareness or ignorance of them. Your thoughtful, conscious choice is the only thing that determines how they work and what is created for you.[5]

> The images you hold in your mind most often will materialize in your life.

There are eight Natural Laws of the Universe, which we will cover in more depth. At first, they may seem complicated, but you'll quickly start to notice the Laws working as you go about your normal daily tasks. Also, since your children are eagerly learning as much as they can to make sense of this big world, they seem to grasp the definitions and concepts more quickly than the parents. After we watch a family movie, our children love to play a game to see how many Laws were represented in the story.

THE EIGHT NATURAL LAWS OF THE UNIVERSE

The Law of Perpetual Transmutation

This Law states that energy moves into and out of physical form.[5]

Everything around you—everything you see, hear, smell, touch, or taste—is energy. The vibration of that energy forms what is seen in the physical world. Everything is in constant motion, and that motion is always changing. Energy cannot be created or destroyed. Instead, it is just moved from one form to another. Like all other forms of energy, our thoughts manifest themselves in the physical world. In other words, what we think about, we bring about. Like water moving to and fro between being a solid, a liquid, or a gas, depending on the temperature (speed of vibration), everything we want or desire moves from our mental thoughts (vibrations) into the physical manifestation of those thoughts, depending on how strongly we believe they will come to be.[5]

> *Part of developing Emotional Intelligence in our children is to give them a broad range of words for their feelings.*

The ideas you hold in your mind are going to happen. They will move into form. When you go out to try something new for the first time, it may be difficult, but when you try again, you are going to find it easier. You've got to keep doing whatever it is you want to do. We can learn that through the use of our Imagination and Memory. We can see ourselves accomplishing goals and building cells of recognition for these achievements. Once you've memorized a picture in your mind and continue to reinforce the image, it moves into form with and through you.[5]

Author Stephen M. R. Covey shares this story from his youth: I remember my dad was teaching us about Habit Two: 'Begin With the End in Mind.' As a family, we drove up to Salt Lake City. He had a friend who was an architect, and we went on top of a really tall building. We looked down from the top of the building into this big hole in the ground right next to our building. What was happening was another building was going up, but it was just a hole at the time.

My dad's friend, who was the architect, pulled out blueprints and said, 'Now look, this building going up; here is this building on the blueprints.' My dad made the point, 'This new building has already been designed; every phase of it, every dimension of it. Every aspect has been designed mentally in the form of this blueprint before it is done physically. What you see right now is just the physical hole, but the building has already been built mentally and on this paper. Now it's going to be executed physically.' This is beginning with the end in mind. You know where you want to go. You decide beforehand; you make your plan. You think it out first then you do it.

We came back a year later and there was a building that was parallel in height to ours. We saw it when it was just a hole in the ground with blueprints. Now we were back there with the architect when he was finishing the thing. That was Dad's lesson on "Beginning With the End in Mind." It was an object lesson; it was real and it was powerful. I remember it to this day.

"Thought is power. Children come out with these fantastical things of what they want to be and do. We never question or dissuade them from that. It is just as easy to dream big as it is to dream small, so why dream small? We tell our children that it's not just that we become what we think about, but we can be anything we want to be. We also tell them we can do whatever we want to do. At their young age they are so impressionable. Every word … they believe you!"[9]

We become what we think about. What is our thought but energy?

The Law of Relativity

Everything is relative. The way we perceive any object, item, person, or idea is always relative to how we see another object, item, person, or idea. There is no big or small, fast or slow, except by comparison.[5]

This Law allows us to gauge what we see. Is someone's life better or worse than ours? It depends on whose life we're comparing to ours. Because of this, no matter where you are in life, there are numerous things to be grateful for now while you work toward what you want. Do you have clean, running water in your home? Many people in this world don't have this luxury that most of us take for granted. Situations don't need to be judged as good or bad; they just are. Therefore, don't dwell on how your situations are not as good as someone else's.[5]

> Any situation can look good or bad, depending on what it is compared to.

"What we are doing as parents is giving our children the markers, the points of reference, by which they compare everything. What you are teaching them is how to judge whether something is good or bad in your life by your reactions. When something comes into our lives, we place a judgment on it based on what our parents have taught us and programmed us to believe. Whether it be what is good and what is bad, what is scary and what is not scary, what is fun and what is boring—those are all things programmed by our parents, and we make a judgment in our own lives, in our own minds, based on those programs. For instance, how do you react to bugs or spiders? Your children are learning whether something is good or bad. If there is a spider crawling across the floor, and you squeal, run, and jump up on a chair, screaming for somebody to come and kill it, your child learns that spiders are bad and that you'd better run for your life because they might take you out.

If you are able to be aware of your reactions, then that can make a huge difference. Our perception is what literally shapes our world into what we see and experience. One person is scared to death of an insect smaller than a quarter, and another sees a cool creature of nature to study. As we are able to change our perception of what is good and what is bad, it completely changes the world that you see around you."[19]

> A perfect example of how the Law of Relativity worked for us was when our son Bradley tripped and fell. There was a split second where he looked at us to choose how to react. Lately, we've been learning that *we want* our children to fall instead of keeping them in a safe little world. We want them to fall down, experience the situation, and learn how to get back up. This teaches them to persevere through mistakes. We could tell that Bradley wasn't bleeding badly, so we said, with excited smiles, "Wow, Bradley! That was just the best fall ever! It was huge! That was awesome!" Immediately, he gave us the biggest smile, and all was okay.

Another time, while driving to South Dakota, we drove through a violent lightening storm. The kids thought the lightening was amazing.

> "Wow! Cool!" Until one bolt was so close to us that the immediate clap of thunder shook the van while we were driving.
>
> Suddenly the kids' chatter changed. "That was scary, Mom!"
>
> "I didn't like that, Dad!"
>
> This was a perfect opportunity for us to teach about the Law of Relativity.
>
> "Oh, I'm not scared! I'm excited! It's so cool to be in the middle of the amazing things that nature can do. This is so not scary!"
>
> Immediately, the chatter went back to "Wow! Did you see that one, Mom?"
>
> "This is so cool!"

Nothing changed on the outside but *everything* changed on the inside.

The Law of Vibration

> Everything vibrates; nothing rests. This Law says that nothing is at rest in the Universe; it's all constantly vibrating. Our awareness of that vibration is what we call feeling. Our feelings are determined by vibration, and we determine our rate of vibration by our thoughts and the paradigms we use to look at life.[5]

"If you look at the space that is around you, it is not empty space, even though it appears to be. It is full of items that are vibrating: the airwaves from telephones, cell phones, radios, TVs, movies. To

 Your children are a mirror of you.

demonstrate this, take a radio and show your child how the knob works and tell them that those are radio waves in the air. Your radio is able to pick up the radio waves because they are all vibrating. The radio attracts the frequency it is aligned with. Whatever station you have it tuned to determines what you will hear."[19] We've used this example to explain this Law to our children. It really helps to show physically what is going on.

Have you ever walked into a room where your children are arguing? The tension is thick and, without thinking, you know that you're going to have to do something to stop the impending fight. Unconsciously, you've just made the decision to change the vibration of the room. "Another great example is when children lie. You can literally see the vibration shrink and go negative when your children lie. You can feel it. Even your pets can feel it and they won't come next to you when you are lying (or angry)."[8]

> A few years ago, we entered into a vicious cycle within our family. The kids went through a phase where they had to test all the rules. We reached a point where all four of our children

were testing us at the same time, and we were getting into a cycle of yelling. We didn't like it, but when we sat back and looked at it, it was just a reflection of us. We yelled, they yelled back, and it continued to escalate. We made a conscious effort to just not yell and instead to talk normally. In fact, we would talk really quietly so they had to lean in to hear us. It totally changed all the dynamics. That whole idea of "your children are a mirror of you" is so true!

Our thoughts consist of vibrations we send out to the Universe. When we focus or concentrate on our thoughts, the vibrations grow stronger. Our awareness of vibration is what we call our feelings. We are in a negative vibration when we say, "Today is going to be a challenge." A positive vibration shows when we say, "I am ready for all the good that today has in store for my family and me!" Since vibration originates with our thoughts, we can control whether we live in a positive or negative vibration. You use your brain to choose which thoughts you'll entertain; it doesn't choose a vibration by itself. You're the master of your thoughts, of your vibration. Your thoughts steer your central nervous system in the direction you choose.[5]

Whether you realize it or not, you've experienced the Law of Vibration within your own family.

Remember, our subconscious mind is a storehouse of images, positive and negative, whichever you allow to take up room there. If you choose to dredge up, examine, and review the bad in life, you move into a negative vibration, and negative feelings immediately follow. The opposite is also true, and if you so choose, you can think positive thoughts, which lead to positive vibrations and will, in turn, put you into a positive mood.[5]

The Law of Attraction

Like attracts like.[5]

This Law is actually secondary to the Law of Vibration because it is our vibrations that cause the attraction. You can't attract what you want in life if you don't know how to control your vibration. Your life has been shaped by what you have attracted over the years. Your thoughts, emotions, and vibrations have attracted everything in your life. Once you are aware of this, you can determine a new course for your life if you do not like your current circumstances. We've met many people with family problems that we know could be improved dramatically if they gained a greater understanding of how much of their results have been caused by their own thinking.[5]

> *You can only attract that which is in harmony with your chosen vibration. Bad moods attract negativity. Great moods attract an abundance of good.*

You draw to yourself the energies that are similar to your own thoughts. The vibrations of the same frequencies attract each other while those of different frequencies repel each other. It is like hitting a tuning fork. If you have a tuning fork with the same frequency near the one you struck, it will begin to vibrate, but forks of different frequencies will not. Have you ever noticed small groups of people who like to gather and just complain about everything in their life? They are drawn together by their similar vibrations. If you are positive about your life, you will find yourself repelled from spending too much time with this negative group and will instead be attracted to positive people.[5]

What is most interesting to us is that we've grown up living according to the Law of Attraction. Whether our parents were aware of it or not, they raised us this way. So many of the phrases that our parents and grandparents have used, like "birds of a feather flock together," "be careful what you wish for," and "give as good as you get" were really just another way of teaching this Law. These Laws have been around forever. Our parents just had different phrases and terminologies.

If you so choose, you can think positive thoughts

You attract the thoughts you focus upon. As you are thinking, you are giving energy to the thoughts, and you create a positive or negative vibration throughout your body. You create your own reality. Let us be blunt. If you think your life stinks, it is your *own fault* for thinking the thoughts you have been thinking. If you don't like what you have attracted in your life, you must change your thoughts to what you want in your life and leave the negative thoughts behind. You can't blame anyone else for what you've got, even though that may be just what you want to do. It has been interesting teaching our children this Law because they want to blame everyone else for their problems. It has taken a lot of time and repetition to undo their thought process, to encourage them to take responsibility for their part in the situation and their thoughts about the situation.[5]

Whatever you want in your life, you must focus on intently. If you dream of riches but only focus on lack and the limitations in your life, you will never achieve financial freedom. By focusing on the negatives such as, "I have no money, and I can't provide a decent life for my children," you barricade your mind from any positive aspects of your abundance. You can't just want something and obsess about not having it. This only creates negative vibrations in the Universe. Take a serious look at the words coming out of your mouth and the internal dialog you have going on in your head. Is it positive or is it negative? If you are truly honest with yourself, you will notice that your thoughts really have given you the circumstances that you have.[5]

Whether you choose to believe this or not does not change the fact that the Law of Attraction is always present and that your existence is a direct result of this and all of the other Laws of the Universe. These Laws have existed since the dawn of time and can't be altered. You do, however, have some control over how you work with them. God gave us free will, and if you consciously choose to create favorable outcomes and work toward those goals, you will create the vibrations that are in harmony with your goals. In turn, these vibrations travel through the Universe, and you attract the life you dream of, not only for yourself, but for your children as well. And, as you model and teach this to your children, they will learn to use the Laws of Vibration and Attraction to bring to them all that they desire.[5]

> *God does not give us a bad situation without also giving us the seed of an equivalent benefit.*

The Law of Polarity

In the Universe, everything has a counterpart that is equal and opposite of itself.[5]

You can't have an up without a down, a good without a bad, or a hot without a cold. There is no such thing as an object with only a left side. A full understanding of this Law will dramatically change how you look at your world and especially how you raise your children. For every mistake your children make, there is a lesson to learn.[5]

The problem is that most people focus on the negative aspects of events. Instead, you *must look for the good* in every event because there is always something good hidden in a bad situation.[5]

> We lost our firstborn child, Tyler, to SIDS when he was only nine weeks old. Fortunately, our faith was strong enough to know that God had a plan for us, even though we didn't know how Tyler's death could possibly fit into this plan. We did know, however, that God is good and that somehow, something positive must come out of this terrible situation. Knowing this helped us through an intense year of grief. Our four other children, Justine, Andrew, Dane, and Bradley, are a result of Tyler's death. We would not have been blessed with the four wonderful kids that we now have had Tyler not died. Our second child, Justine, is the only girl on Cory's side of the family of seven grandchildren. At the time, we could not have known what good was to come out of our son's death, but we did not focus on the negative. We kept our minds focused on the positive, which made all the difference.

The Law of Polarity gives us an opportunity to pause and think about every occurrence that we experience in life. When something happens, we have a choice to look at it as a good event or a bad situation. When we interview parents about their family life, we often hear them say, "It is what it is." This is actually a good thought because we need to realize that everything "just is." Because of the Laws of Polarity and Relativity, all of your "it's" are both good and bad, depending on what you compare "it" to. As humans, we seem drawn to find the bad in everything. Unfortunately, most people don't take the next step and look for the good in the situation.

Try this experiment: if a person is complaining about something, come back at them with a positive response to their negative comment. This is interesting because it completely shifts their perspective. They are somewhat caught off guard. Your positive energy removed their negative energy.

You need to take every bad situation and tell yourself that there is something good that will come of this. Then, actively look for the lesson or good situation that comes as a result of the bad. We have the privilege of interpretation, so we can choose to view any situation as a positive or a negative. From that choice, we set vibration in motion, our vibration determines our feelings, and our feelings drive our actions and results. Find that seed of equivalent benefit in every situation, and the good results will follow.[5]

> **When you're looking for gold, you go through tons of dirt, but you don't focus on the dirt, you focus on the gold!**

"We learned and taught our kids that when we have a pitfall or some bad news that, just around the corner, is something equally, oppositely amazing or even better.

When things have gone really horrible, or they have had a bad day, we like to say, 'You know what? There is this Law of Polarity thing that says, you can count on this: that since this was really, really horrible, there is something amazing that can come from it. Let's keep our eyes open and look for it.'

They become excited, and then we, too, become excited. Now when something is really, really bad, our daughter will start looking, 'Where is the good? If something is bad, there has got to be good, too.'"[23]

If you can just train your children to be aware that both sides exist, it will change their entire experience. Author Leslie Householder's favorite Law of Polarity story involves two little boys. One of them sees all this manure everywhere.

He says, "What kind of a Christmas is this with all this poop everywhere! This is awful! This is the most horrible Christmas I have ever had!" he whines through his tears.

The other one is romping in it and tossing it around. He is having so much fun.

"What on earth are you doing?" the mother asks.

"With all this poop, there has got to be a pony around somewhere!" Our kids love that story. Sometimes, we will bring it up and remind them that there is just a lot of poop around, so let's go find what is good.

People around us constantly say, "How can you be so positive?" Simple. We believe in the Law of Polarity and when something really bad happens in your life, if you are looking for the good instead of wallowing in self-pity, God places something just as good or better in your life. Remember, when you're looking for gold, you go through tons of dirt, but you don't focus on the dirt; you focus on the gold!

The Law of Rhythm

Our Universe moves in a repetitive rhythm. Day to night, low tide to high tide, winter to spring, summer, and fall. These patterns in life help to balance us.[5]

The Law of Rhythm is frequently discussed at our house. Bradley was getting ready for bed, and it was still a little bit light out.

"It's getting really dark!" he said.

"Yeah, it's getting really dark. That's what happens. The sun sets and it is shining on the other side of the world. In the morning the sun will be shining on our side of the world again. That happens every day. It happens because of the Law of Rhythm. There is a rhythm to it, and it does it every day. It is always going to happen."[19]

"There are other opportunities to teach this Law. We encourage you to just talk to your children about everything. When we go out for walks, we see the different trees; there are leaf-bearing trees, which are deciduous trees, and the pine trees, which are coniferous trees. We just talk about what we see and relate that visual example to how the laws work.

> 'See these trees right here? Let's watch them through the next couple of months. In the wintertime, they don't have any leaves.'
>
> Talk to your child about how, in another couple months, they are going to have leaves. As the summer comes, say, 'Look at the beautiful leaves on the trees.'
>
> As it turns to fall, say, 'See the leaves changing colors? Soon, the leaves will fall off. Then winter comes again.'"[19]

Just talk to them about how that is the Law of Rhythm. There is a rhythm to the earth.

> *Our moods have a natural rhythm of ups and downs.*

It is important to realize that we aren't going to feel great all of the time; no one does. If we did, would we even know when we were happy? The valleys allow us to enjoy the peaks in our lives. There will always be highs and lows in life. Fortunately, Reason gives us the ability to choose our thoughts. (We'll discuss Reason in greater detail in the next chapter.) It is important for us to remember that even when we are on a natural downswing, we can choose positive and encouraging thoughts. When we notice we are in a low spot, we need to use our reasoning ability to help us remember that this low will not last forever, and that we will soon start on an upswing as we begin to move toward a high. We can even speed up this process of moving to a high. When you realize that you are in a low spot, consciously begin thinking about something good. If you have a setback on your way toward a goal, stop, visualize, and feel yourself as you will be when you reach your goal.[5]

Flip your switch from negative to positive thoughts. We realize that when you are in a low place, it is much more difficult to think optimistic thoughts. However, even if you only take a short amount of time, say 20 seconds, when you begin to think of something good and happy, you move your vibration to a more positive state. This small increase brings to you other positive thoughts, which, in turn, take you to an even higher level. Through the repetitive nature of thinking positive thoughts, even in small increments, you continue to move to higher and higher levels of vibration, and you work your way out of the low you are in.[5]

Since you already know that a high follows this low because of the rhythmic nature of the Universe, why not move yourself to the high even faster? What a powerful tool to pass on to your children! When they learn to notice when they are in a negative state and can change their thoughts and work themselves to a happier state, they feel empowered and have control over their emotions and their lives.

The Law of Cause and Effect

For every action, there is an equal and opposite reaction.[5]

What you send out into the Universe comes back. Everything in the Universe is subject to Universal Laws, and everything that happens does so because it was caused.[5] This is very evident in the way we raise our children. If we don't teach them to be leaders or to be imaginative, we end up with children who are followers and are prone to get into trouble.

"Our kids can recite Newton's Law from science: *For every action, there is an equal and opposite reaction.* Not only can they recite it, they know what it means. We teach them because we are such proponents of that Law."[9] But in practical terms, how do you teach that when you are parenting? "'Your actions have consequences. Look, this is what is going to happen if you do this.' Oftentimes when we need to leave the house, there is one child who doesn't want to put his or her shoes on, so we offer a choice: 'Okay, you can put your shoes on, or we're going to help you put your shoes on. It is your choice.' This is really effective because the child doesn't feel bossed around. You're putting the child in charge of his or her life, which is so important for confidence and self-esteem."[9]

In each area of your life, develop positive statements you can repeat in your mind regularly. It is through repetition that we replace old habits of thoughts with new, positive thought habits.

Many of us know this Law as the Golden Rule: "Do unto others, as you would have them do unto you." We use this Law in moments of bad behavior but also good behavior. "If you do good things, good things happen to you, too. If you do something bad, bad things come back to you. If you do stay focused on doing good, then good things generally happen." We speak to them like little adults because that is what they are. Their minds have infinite capacity to absorb. Parents often forget or perhaps don't understand this. Even our minds as adults have *infinite* capacity to absorb. We must never underestimate it in young people.[5]

> *Luck, chance, and accidents don't exist.*

Our actions during our parenting years greatly affect whether or not our children are successful. The way we get the results we want is by working on the cause behind those results. ***A changed cause must produce a changed effect.*** One way to change your cause is to focus on it, using positive affirmations to point you in the direction you wish to go. In each area of your life, develop positive statements you can repeat in your mind regularly. It is through repetition that we replace old habits of thoughts with new, positive thought habits. These affirmations should be in the present tense, carefully crafted to focus you on what you really want. Whatever you send into the Universe comes back.[5] We often tell our children, "If you don't have anything nice to say, just don't say it." But what about the thoughts you are having about other people? What about the thoughts you have about yourself? Say good words to everyone, including yourself; treat everyone with total respect, and your thoughts turn more positive. It all comes back to you. Remember, sometimes we think a door is shut because something has happened to us. That is the cause. You get to control the effect. You get to control what happens on the other end. We want to create thinking children who can think for themselves and who can make decisions.

The Law of Gestation

Every seed has a gestation or incubation period and everything in the Universe has a masculine and feminine side.[5]

The principle of both male and female in the entire Universe makes potential, regeneration, and motion possible. This is evident in nature. We plant an acorn, and soon we have an oak sapling. You wouldn't plant an acorn and expect tomatoes to sprout instead, right? The same is true for ideas. Just as every

> *You must have faith that your ideas and goals are moving into the physical.*

acorn that is planted in the ground begins to move toward becoming an oak tree, every idea that is given energy begins to move into the physical world. You must remember that ideas, like oak trees, take time to manifest. ***Don't dig up your ideas to see if they are growing roots or you will surely kill any sprout that may have started.***[5]

"The Law of Gestation teaches patience. Our kids have seen us set goals, only to see them come true much later than expected. As parents, the best way for us to demonstrate this is through our own lives. Be patient and focus on your intentions. Teaching children the gestation period is hard to do. But if you live it, talk about it, and hold on until your goals are achieved, then point it out to them by saying, 'Aren't we glad that this didn't happen back when we thought it should have because look how it would have affected everything else?' Parents have the capability to put a positive spin on the delay; this teaches children to have more patience in their own goals."[23]

Just having the knowledge of how the Natural Laws of the Universe operate will be of no benefit to you unless you consciously work with them.

We set a goal in our early 20s, to have a big, beautiful grandfather clock. We had no idea how we were going to make it happen. We wrote the goal on several different vision boards, but after a while, it became less of a priority. When our grandmother passed away, we received about a $10,000 inheritance and decided to use the money to get a grandfather clock in memory of her. It was so fabulous because the price was no longer an issue, so we got to pick any clock we wanted. This is such a perfect example of the Law of Gestation because that clock took 18 years to be attracted. Not once did we think, "We're never going to get our grandfather clock." We just kept saying, "We're going to get it someday." Sure enough, it showed up. It's probably the longest gestation period we have ever had for anything.

Each goal has a given gestation period, and if you continue to nurture your goals by visualizing them with emotion and by taking action toward those goals, your goals develop into what you want. We do not know what the gestation periods are for our goals, but they *will* manifest when the time is right.[5]

We hope you learn to harmonize and align with the Universal Laws in order to help your children create the lives that they deserve. By discovering and implementing these Laws in your daily lives, you also teach your children to do the same. Remember this, however: just having the knowledge of how the Natural Laws of the Universe operate will be of no benefit to you unless you consciously work with them. Having unwavering certainty in these Laws allows and enables you to experience a life above and beyond your wildest dreams. Do these Laws make the events and circumstances in your life clearer to you?

ACTION STEPS

Go through each of the Natural Laws of the Universe and write down a time when you knowingly or unknowingly used them to teach your children.

The Law of Perpetual Transmutation

The Law of Relativity

The Law of Vibration

The Law of Attraction

The Law of Polarity

The Law of Rhythm

The Law of Cause and Effect

The Law of Gestation

For more writing space please visit
www.ParentOutLoud.com/STEP to download your free PlayBook.

CHAPTER 6

EXPANDING YOUR WALLS

*If you can conceive it in your mind, then it can
be brought to the physical world.*

–Bob Proctor

"Dane, did you hear your little voice talking to you when you were stealing your big sister's candy?"

"Yes," the five-year-old calmly replied.

"What did it say?" Anamarie asked.

"It said I shouldn't do it."

"Why didn't you listen to your little voice?" she said.

"Because my sweet tooth hasn't fallen out yet." He delivered this statement with such calm conviction that Anamarie had to turn away, struggling to hold back her laughter.

"Your sweet tooth was talking to you?" she said.

"It talks as loud as a computer game, and my little voice only whispers!"

The next day Anamarie inquired further.

"Dane. Just where is your sweet tooth?"

He opened his mouth and pointed to a tooth. "It's right here." Then he pointed to a different tooth, "And I have one here, and here, and here."

"Wow, you have four sweet teeth! No wonder you couldn't hear your little voice!"

The Anchor Bolts

Just like anchor bolts firmly connect a house's framing to the concrete footings of the foundation, you have Six Higher Intellectual Faculties, which link your mind to the life-changing power of living in harmony with the Eight Natural Laws of the Universe. These Intellectual Faculties, or "mental muscles," are the creative faculties, which separate us from all of the other creatures on our planet. Organized educational institutions do a great job at requiring the use of one faculty, Memory, although they don't actually teach us *how* to memorize. Additionally, our educational system does not teach us how to recognize and develop any of our other faculties. Education focuses on memory work for kids to recite answers during tests. Our children aren't really using their brains to think. And most adults aren't using their brains to think, either. We may think we are thinking but if you actually take a look at most of your actions, they are just habitual behaviors. Do you remember when you learned to drive? You had

Parents who teach their children the Natural Laws of the Universe prepare them for success.

to consciously think about the steering wheel, gas pedal, brake, blinkers, mirrors, etc. Fast forward ten years and all of those tasks have become habit. Do you remember the last time you drove home and really didn't remember how you got there because your mind was on something completely different? You followed your normal habit of driving home without thinking.[5]

> *Our Intellectual Faculties give us the ability to think, transform, and create the life we desire.*

We are all born with five senses: sight, taste, touch, hearing, and smell. By the age of five, most children have a complete understanding of their ability to use their five senses to understand the world and environment around them. The five senses are amazing gifts that are very important, but they are limited to telling us and showing us what already is and have no power to create or transform. This is why our Intellectual Faculties are so important.[5]

They are present in each and every one of us, and each faculty identifies a powerful area of thought that we can actually use to change our habits and transform our lives. The six Higher Intellectual Faculties are:

1. Will: the ability to focus your attention on one item.
2. Imagination: the ability to create mental pictures.
3. Perception: the ability to see different points of view.
4. Reason: the ability to think, use logic, and gather information.
5. Intuition: the ability to pick up other's energy.
6. Memory: the ability to recall information.

Thinking Outside The Box

We all possess these higher faculties, but that does not mean that we all utilize them to the best of our abilities. Our friend Orrin Hudson says, "In this life, you have to be amazing! Excellence is not enough. Being excellent will get only get you so far. You'll get laid off for being excellent and promoted for being amazing. People will stand in line three hours and get rid of a cell phone that is excellent just to buy an iPhone. What does it take to be amazing? You've got to go above and beyond. You've got to do more than you're supposed to do. You've got to arrive early. You've got to stay late. You have to delight people. You have to blow them away. You have to be fabulous." But most of all, you have to use your Intellectual Faculties in every aspect of your life.

> *Just like your physical muscles,*
> *your mental muscles must be exercised if you are to*
> *keep them strong and fit.*

The difference between people who are excellent and amazing is the comprehension of the importance of the Intellectual Faculties. These faculties are areas that most people don't even think about, and therefore they do not know that they are missing out on utilizing some of the most important tools that can be used to improve our lives and in turn the lives of our children. The ability to make sound decisions is directly related to the development, integration, and strength of these six faculties which, when exercised, expand infinitely.[5]

Because your ability to have the life of your dreams starts with your decisions, it is critical for you to continue to build and strengthen these mental muscles. Let's take a closer look at each one of these six faculties.

The Will

In the truest sense, The Will enables us to *hold an image, idea, or thought* that we want in our conscious mind until it embeds itself into our subconscious. This is important because it is through our subconscious that our thoughts manifest in our lives. If we want to change something in our life, we can use our Will to take any subconscious idea that may have been present in our minds since childhood and replace it with the idea we want. We can do this through intense concentration, with repetition in the form of affirmations, and over time, we "will" the idea we want into being. This new idea replaces the old one that we inherited from our parents or society.[5]

Many times, The Will is confused with stubbornness. "In the early 1950s, the leading thought and teachings of the day, as far as raising children was concerned, was that you had to break the will of the child. In addition to that, everyone was afraid of spoiling their child. The theory at that time was, 'Don't spoil your child. If the child is crying, don't pick the child up. You'll spoil the child if you give him or her too much attention.' Parents thought they were doing right by breaking the will of their child.

Consequently, we have many parents who are now functioning as *broken adults*. This affects every aspect of your life because it affects your belief in yourself. It is from our beliefs that we create our outward world and accomplish the goals we can achieve. This is a serious problem. But now, we have all kinds of new insights: we have better doctors and better writers out there teaching about the newly discovered research. The problem is that a lot of the people who were damaged as kids have grown up; however, they are not reading these new informational books, and these old beliefs are still getting passed down from generation to generation because this is the how they were raised. They think the way they were raised is the right way to raise their kids."[30]

When parenting children, it can be very helpful to approach The Will as "what are they willing to do and what are they not willing to do?" Many times we think our children are being "willful" when all they really want is to make their own choices. Our friend Roxie Griego shared this story:

> Kids always have chores. I personally like my chores done in the morning. I like beds made, things put away and tidied up, the dishes in the dishwasher before leaving for work and school so I don't have to come home to a mess. Everybody has chores in the morning. But one of my children was not willing to do them. Why? She was a willful child, and she didn't like getting up early because she's a night person. But you know what she was willing to do? She was willing to do her chores after her homework was finished. She got them done beautifully so in the morning if she wanted to sleep that extra hour instead of having to get up and go through the rat race like everyone else was willing to do, she didn't have to get up, hurry to take a bath, get dressed, get her chores done, and then get out the door. Her chores were done the night before because she was willing to do so. This made a big difference in our mornings because she was willing to do the chore at a different time, and we gave her the freedom to do it. A peaceful agreement is much better than a tension-filled house.

We have to reject the old habit and consciously work to replace it with a new habit we want.

One of the traits of highly successful people is a strong Will. "We have had generations of squashing The Will of our children. 'We don't want willful children. We want quiet, obedient children.' It's time we outgrow that paradigm. Our children are going to have an extraordinary life because we teach them all the time that their Will is so important. The Will determines what we think and what we hold onto and what we believe. Any habit that we want to stop or change must encounter our Will. The term *will power* has been used in conjunction with weight loss, addiction, and exercise, but it can also be used to stop habitual thoughts and negative self-doubt."[30]

Imagination

Imagination is our creative power. Great minds have created and invented numerous things ranging from artificial hearts to the Internet, against all doubts and odds because of the power of imagination in combination with the other intellectual skills. As parents, we're helping to build great minds. The only way that our children are going to invent things that don't exist is by helping them to create something in their minds first. Help your children develop that skill daily. Since they are already playing, we don't have to help them play; just encourage their imaginations. One of the reasons we love our kids so much is their imagination.

> **Any situation can look good or bad depending on what it is compared against.**

> When we have dinner or play games on Friday nights, we're amazed at the creative things they say. One night, they asked us what it would be like if we were all made out of Lego bricks. Instead of telling them how ridiculous that sounded, we played along and talked about how you'd have to take off your legs when you took off your pants. We all laughed at the thought of a closet filled with Lego legs and we spent the next 30 minutes talking about what else could happen.

Imagination not only gives us laughs but creates a bonding time for our family as well. Imagination is a lot of fun for the entire family. We can't envision our children not having or exploring their imagination. One of the most important places to expand this faculty is on the playground because their brains develop to their fullest potential as a result of being outside, learning social skills, being creative, and entertaining themselves, instead of being entertained by TV or video games. Imagination is where a seed is planted, and you tell children to find and follow their dreams. They need to expand their minds by thinking and asking questions like, "What else is out there?" "How can I do it differently?" Do you ever wonder why kids understand the concept of goal setting so much better than adults? They don't have the jaded viewpoint of what can and can't be done. As adults, we have a more strongly formed ego that argues with doing and trying new things. Our disappointments, betrayals, and challenges can cause us to be very cynical. But a child hasn't experienced these emotions so they are eager to try new things. If we instill an active imagination in our children, they'll retain the natural curiosity that we are all born with as well as a vivid imagination.

So much of goal setting and accomplishing our dreams in life has to do with the power of imagination. How can we see ourselves differently, and how can we move in the direction of what we see and who we need to become in order to manifest the school, job, or the partner we would like to have for our children? All that is easier because they don't have to unlearn old and outdated beliefs passed down to them.

Expanding your mind to what else is out there is important because there is so much more that our physical senses can't see. Everything that has been created was first created in someone's imagination. Nothing can be made without the maker seeing the image of the creation first on the screen of their mind. When applied to your actions, your imagination is either creating how you can do something or why you can't. Sadly, we raise our children with the idea that some people are creative and some people are not. That is not true. Everybody is creative.

Perception

It was a cold January morning in Washington, DC—peak hour in a busy metro station as commuters rushed to work. A man dressed in jeans and baseball cap pulled out his violin and played six Bach pieces for about 45 minutes, an amazing sound with surprisingly good acoustics.

Three minutes passed before a middle-aged man noticed the music and slowed down for a few seconds, then rushed off to meet his schedule. Moments later the violinist received his first dollar tip from a woman who threw the money in his violin case as she continued on her way. Another gentleman stopped to listen, but not for long; a glance at his watch had him taking off quickly. The most enthusiastic listener was a three-year-old boy; several other children were mesmerized but dragged away by busy parents.

For the 45-minute duration, only six people stopped and listened for a while. About 20 contributed to a total of $32. The music stopped; it was silent again, and no one noticed. No one applauded; there was no recognition. For no one knew that the violinist was Joshua Bell, one of the best musicians in the world! He'd been playing one of the most intricate pieces of music ever written, on a violin worth $3.5 million. Two days earlier, he'd played to a full house in a Boston theatre, where tickets averaged $100.00. What a contrast!

You see, Joshua Bell had agreed to take part in a social experiment organized by the *Washington Post* to understand ordinary people's perception, taste, and priorities. In a commonplace environment at an inappropriate hour, did they perceive beauty or appreciate it? Did they recognize talent in an unexpected context? *No!*

Isn't it interesting that it was the small children who knew something special was happening? They were "in the present moment," not bothered by time.

Perception creates meaning from events or experiences in our life. We interpret these based on past events and programming. In relation to perception, everything is relative. Nothing has meaning, or is good or bad, until we think it so. Consequently, each person has a different perception or interpretation of exactly the same event or object. We often hear stories of police officers interviewing several witnesses of an accident, and every single person has a different story. This is entirely due to each person's different perceptions of the event. In the middle of a life-saving surgery, it would appear that a murder has occurred in the room. Remember, there are always two sides to a story. For instance, when children have a disagreement, we have to see the disagreement from the each child's perspective, which sometimes isn't all that easy.[5]

You teach them how to judge whether something is good or bad in your life by your reactions.

For example, our youngest son ate his brother's jellybeans. When they were arguing, we had to make Bradley understand that he shouldn't have eaten the candy without asking, and at the same time, we had to tell Dane that he needed to share. We wanted to show each of the boys both sides of the argument. That is not always easy to do because children always think their point of view is correct. Trying to look through someone else's eyes is a very difficult skill, which is made easier by showing them each other's viewpoint.

Part of what our job is as parents is to show our children all of the sides of a situation that we can see but that they have not yet learned to understand through personal experience. Pointing out all the other ways that you can look at a situation can seriously expand your children's minds. A great perception exercise we've done with our kids is to ask them to close their eyes and imagine something big. Then we continue to paint a picture in their mind's eye:

"If you walked up to it and you put your hand flat on it, you couldn't tell if it was the top or the bottom. What is this? It's flat but kind of curvy. What is this? It feels scratchy. It feels kind of wrinkly on your left side. Scratchy on the left side and it is wrinkly on the right side. You put your face to it and it is warm. Actually, it is kind of soft. Then you put your nose to it and it smells really, really bad. However, you open your eyes and you say to yourself, 'Gosh, is that grey? It looks black but I think it's grey. It's not quite brown.' Then you start stepping away from it. Start imagining what it might look like when you step away from it and you are actually looking at an elephant. You can't appreciate it when it's that close up because it's scratchy and warm and it stinks and it's kind of brown and grey. As you step back and look at the whole thing and you say, 'Wow! What a cool animal! That's an elephant.'[31]

> *Never underestimate the role of perception*
> *in our daily lives.*

It's critical to constantly be aware of Perception. It colors every moment of our days. "You can be up close and personal and not get it. You can step back and take another look at it and think, 'Wow, I get it!'"[31] How you look at life determines your results. When you change the way you look at life, your life changes. See the good in everything. Don't look at the outside pictures. See what you want to see in your mind and perceive what you would have it be in your perfect world. Look at everything as good. How much happier would our children be if we could teach them to see the good in all things? How much better would our world be?

Perception has the power to alter our attitude and course of direction almost without our notice. It takes much strength of will to change perceptions we have held for a long time.[5]

Reasoning

Reasoning is our ability to understand the events in our world. We need to teach our children to think. Thinking can be taught just the same as you can teach typing or playing a piano.[5] When children are really small, reasoning is not as easy. If you ask children to think, "What is your reason behind a particular feeling or behavior?" you are giving them an opportunity to learn how to think. Reading to your children is a great way to teach them reasoning skills because they have to filter the information they're hearing, understand its meaning, and then decide if it is right or wrong. They tend to participate more, ask more questions, and take an active part in conversations. Provoke their thoughts by asking questions.

> "'What is reasonable here? Is this the way we should do this, or should we do it this way? We have two different choices here. If we do this one, what will happen?'
>
> 'Then, let's take it a step further ... and then what?'
>
> Anytime they make a decision, the next step is to ask, 'And then what is going to happen? ... and after that, then what's going to happen ...' to where they are thinking three or four steps down the road. We also want to teach them how to reason out *why* they made a particular decision by asking, 'Why do you believe that? What do you mean by that? Why do you say that? Why did that come out at this time? How did you come to that conclusion?' We want to challenge them to understand that we, as parents, want to know where they are getting their ideas from and if they are reasonable."[18]

Reasoning also helps us impress upon our kids that every child wants to be right all the time. We believe it is important to displace that with a humility that says, "You know what? I don't have to be right all the time." "Kids develop reasoning by letting them make the wrong decision, and most importantly, you have to let your kids fail! You can't fix their problems. You can't call the parents and say, 'You're daughter did this to my baby!' You can't call the teacher and say, 'My daughter doesn't deserve that grade.' Instead say 'Honey, I'm sorry you got a D in math. Why do you think that happened?'"[8]

Have you ever had a great idea and when someone asked you where it came from you responded, "I don't know, it just came to me out of thin air." Thoughts are constantly surrounding you. It's like standing in a grocery that's fully stocked; the ingredients are always there. But you can't make a recipe if everything sits on the shelves. You have to go get the ingredients and put them together to make a recipe. The same is true with thoughts; your mind collects them and they mix with your beliefs. All you have to do is put them together to create something meaningful.

If our children spend too many years acting like someone else, they soon forget that they are pretending.

Help your children understand that there is a magnificent power flowing through them. It's an invisible power, and they can make thoughts out of it, and then can put them together and make ideas. Reasoning is required to develop their thinking skills.[5] "Let's sit down. We are going to talk about this. We are going to reason through it, and we are going to find some common ground here."[31]

When you are not using your reasoning skills, you will quickly reject anything that doesn't match your current understanding or paradigms. This guarantees that you continue to act on ideas that keep that paradigm in place. Unfortunately, this is likely to cause you to reject an idea that would move your life forward.[5]

If you don't have good reasoning skills, you stay in your comfort zone, and your surrounding environment creates your attitudes. An example would be when you find your mood worsening because your children aren't listening to you. When you are angry or frustrated at your children, stop and question why you are letting their behavior alter your behavior. Use your reasoning to calmly help guide your children through the situation rather than reacting out of anger or frustration.

Intuition

Often referred to as our "sixth sense," intuition is our ability to connect with other individuals without even knowing or speaking to them. When we meet someone who immediately makes us feel good or positive, our intuition senses the positive energy that person projects. When we meet someone who makes us feel negative or scared, our intuition immediately warns us of their negativity. Our children have all known from an early age that they can talk to God, that he answers prayers, and this communication is in the form of intuition and inner knowing.[5]

> *Many spiritual leaders have said that prayer is "us speaking to God" and intuition is "God speaking to us."*

Everything we do today is going to affect all of our tomorrows. Intuition is for really listening to our own personal thought process about what is going on in our heads for any given situation, whether it is playing with someone you know who isn't a good influence or someone who is. Check in. Do you feel like they are really a good influence on you? Are you really listening to what is going on in your head and in your heart?[5]

> Whenever our children make a mistake or whenever they are in trouble, we point out to them, "Right before you did that, did you have a little voice or feeling inside of you saying that it probably wasn't such a good idea but you did it anyway?"

"Yeah."

"Well, okay, you know what that is? That's your intuition telling you that you knew better. You knew better than to do it and you did it anyway. You always have that little voice inside of you and it's so important to listen to it. Your intuition is right 100 percent of the time."

With kids, just making them aware of their intuition helps them to tap into it at an early age and learn to trust it even more as an adult. So many times, many parents want to tell their children what to do rather than let them to think for themselves what to do. Teaching them *how* to tune into their intuition means telling them that they have to learn how to get quiet and listen to what they have going on in their head and in their gut. We all have this fantastic intuition, and we just don't give it enough time to speak loud enough to our ears, but it is there. Teach your kids to check their gut feelings and then tell them to ask themselves, "Do I feel like this friend is really a good influence on me? They'll soon find out whether or not they're listening to their intuition.

We have to reject the old habit and consciously work to replace it with a new habit we want.

Developing your intuition in order to tune in to the highest level of those around you allows you to see through all the noise of conversation, and immediately understand the essence of who they are and what they are about.

Memory

Memory is our ability to recall previous events and experiences. Many of us tend to remember only our failures, and those memories seem to linger much longer and be more intense than memories of our successes. It is important to use our memory to bolster our confidence and self-esteem as we try something new.[5] A book that came highly recommended to us is *The Memory Book*.

We were able to take a concept from the second chapter and help our daughter create ridiculous image associations to memorize a really long Bible verse that she had to learn in order to go on a church field trip. We watched her memorize this in 15 minutes! It was phenomenal to watch her do this, all because we created this silly little mental movie that she was able to walk herself through, and she just spouted off the sentences. The next time she needed to memorize something she came back.

What society says doesn't matter. You are the ruler of your life.

"Let's do that game again because I need to memorize this ...." We loved coming up with the goofy pictures. I read the verse and she creates an image.

"Oh that is so not goofy enough! It's got to be sillier than that."

So she got even weirder describing the visual image.

"Now are you going to remember that?" we asked. And she smiled.

One of the most important traits all successful people have is memory, in particular the ability to remember people's names. "We teach our kids memory games so they can easily remember people they've met. If there is someone in our life whom we want to remember, we ask our kids, 'What was that person wearing? Tell us their name or something about them.' We always drill the importance of memory into our kids' heads because that is the first piece of information we would need to know in a serious situation. This is not only a fun game but a skill for later in life, too."[2]

Celebrate Your Success

Consciously focusing on past success, no matter how small, improves our overall self-confidence. Every person reading this book has succeeded in multiple areas of life to get to this point. Claim those successes and remember them every time you set your course for a new journey in life. One of the best ways we've found to claim our successes are through a dream/success journal. A dream/success journal is a special journal where you write all your successes and achievements.

> In our journal, we take pictures from magazines or books and attach them to pages along with a phrase and date. For example, we want a new house, so we searched through countless home magazines and found the one we wanted. After we glued it to the page, we wrote, "I am so happy and grateful for my new home," and dated the top of the page. Our success/dream journal is filled with every one of our goals. We carry it with us everywhere we go and read it on a daily basis. This practice puts the images in our subconscious mind so they can soon be a reality. We also make a spreadsheet and include all of our accomplishments on it, no matter how big or small. It is just as important for our children to acknowledge their successes as it is for us. One way to acknowledge *their* success is to teach them to keep a dream/success journal as well.

We recommend writing at least five successes each day. Look at your child's triumphs to see if there is a correlation between them and one of the higher faculties. Did your child get a better grade on a project at school because of imagination? Were they able to protect a friend from danger by the use of reasoning? The most important aspect to remember regarding this journal is to keep your focus on success! Success breeds success. Success attracts more success. The dream/success journal also assists you when the going gets tough. It reminds you of your strength and capability to overcome challenges in your life. Acknowledge and celebrate your success!

Some parents may find it difficult to teach these Higher Faculties and their relation to success to their children because only a very small percentage of the population understands the correlation. The best way to show your children this is to turn these faculties into family conversations. Say, "This is interesting stuff!" When you are learning it, you are also doing it. What we are doing is learning how and why, so as parents, share these higher faculties with your kids through examples. Remember that young people and older people are all the same people because there is only one mind. If we can understand that and quit the baby talk with little kids and talk to them like we would talk to our next-door neighbor, then we can give our children the tools to succeed. The only things children are missing are vocabulary and experience. Take that into consideration when you are talking to them because *you* provide the vocabulary, and *life* provides the experience.

ACTION STEPS

Review each one of the Intellectual Faculties and find a situation in your family or child's life that you can apply them to.

1. Will

2. Imagination

3. Perception

4. Reasoning

5. Intuition

6. Memory

Have family members create their own dream/success journal.

Link how one or more of the higher faculties and Universal Laws contributed to their success.

Write five successes daily in your journal.

For more writing space please visit
www.ParentOutLoud.com/STEP to download your free PlayBook.

CHAPTER 7

INSULATION

Since the house is on fire, let us warm ourselves.

-Italian Proverb

"Well, I will let you talk to his father, Officer." Jonathan's mother hands the phone to her husband, Richard. He stares at the clock striking midnight as he absorbs the officer's words.

"Your son has been pulled over for excessive speeding. He was traveling 83 miles per hour in a 25 mph zone. There was no alcohol or drugs involved. He seems like a good kid who just had an episode of poor teenage judgment."

When things had calmed the next day, Jonathan said, "Well, Dad, I was just trying to get home for curfew, so I had to go really fast to make it."

"So let me see if I understand. Last month, we came up with an agreement; we were happy to let you drive and use the family car. We even paid for the insurance. We emphasized that driving is a privilege, not a right. And we went over the rules together: be safe, drive within the speed limits, wear your seatbelt, and obey the laws. You told us, 'Yeah, I've got it Mom; got it, Dad.' We asked if you were clear on these rules, because if you violated them you would lose the privilege to drive. I remember you saying, 'Don't worry!' We clarified our expectations and extended our trust to you. Am I understanding the situation correctly?"

The young Jonathan twisted his hands, "Yes, Dad."

"So now we have to hold you accountable. We're going to play this thing out. And you will have to behave your way out of this problem that you behaved your way in to."

Several weeks later, the family went to court. The judge fined Jonathan $555, and he had to pay the fine with all of his savings from his summer job. That was hard on him, but what happened next was even harder. The judge did not suspend his license. So his parents did suspend his license. Why? They wanted Jonathan to trust them. After having all those conversations about the privilege of driving, laying out the rules, and setting the expectation that rule violation results in loss of privileges, they felt that by not following through and not suspending his license would violate the trust between the children and their parents. This experience was very embarrassing with his friends and was even harder on the family because they lost their extra driver.

After a couple of months Jonathan came into his dad's office.

"Dad, I'm ready to drive again."

"Are you clear on the rules?"

"Dad, I've never been more clear about anything in my life."[34]

What's Your R-Value?

In life, we often question who we are and what our place is in this world. These are particularly important questions for us as individuals but even more as parents. How we define ourselves, whether it is by race, gender, nationality, religion, ethnicity, community, or status greatly affects our children. The purpose of insulation in a home is to keep the inside living space comfortable. It does so by resisting the weather outside. The thermal resist is the R-Value rating; the higher the number, the greater its resisting power. Just like insulation, it's parents' responsibility to create a comfortable home environment for our children in which to grow and thrive.

Over the past several decades, there have been many changes in society that have influenced our belief systems. Violence and sex not only bombard our kids today through the media, Internet, and video games, but glorify it as well. The relationship between parent and child is essential to teaching the importance of character and values.

> If, for example, a son grows up in a household where his father shows respect to his mother, he will be more likely to treat his spouse in the same manner. Our children identify not only with their mother and father as separate individuals but with the relationship between them.

The example we set as parents paints the canvas that our children carry into adulthood. We can color their world with unwavering faith and a strong set of values or smudge it with uncertainty. Faith and values aren't instantaneous. We can't just download them onto our children like we do with a song on iTunes. Instead, faith and values are a lifetime journey of self-discovery, critical thinking, deepening commitments, and trusting relationships.

Understanding this is important for parents who want to teach their children to live according to their own convictions in today's challenging environment.

We see so many people constantly chasing success, yet many never seem satisfied with what they currently have. Imagine the effect this has on their children. The children watch their parents chase elusive goals day after day and listen to them complain about their present situation. You have to be happy and grateful with where you currently are in your life. If you aren't, then you're setting an example for your children that happiness isn't possible, and it depends upon something that you don't have. This causes personal happiness to always elude you. If your life is a mess, you have to realize that all of your past actions have brought you to where you are today. You may have goals for more, and that is great! But if you continuously complain about what you now have, the Universe will not reward you with more. Realize that no matter how bad it may seem to you, there is always something for which you can be grateful, even if it is just knowing that you have access to clean running water, which is something that not everyone in this world has.

Gauge your success based on your own life.

Now, for a quick assessment of where you are: take a look around you at the rooms in your home. Are they neat and tidy, or do you have toys on the floor, piles of papers that need to be filed, and dishes in the sink? Are you financially secure or living paycheck to paycheck? Do you get along with your spouse and children, or do you bicker constantly? Maybe all those things are fine, but is there still something that you aren't happy with in your life. Your actions in the past have created this reality, but your actions going forward can change your future reality. Be grateful for what you have and take a serious look at your life, take responsibility for where you are today, and know that if you don't like what you see, you have the power to make a change.

Have you ever taken the time to sit down and define what truly makes you happy? Perhaps if you defined what success really means to you, then you would have a parameter against which to judge your success. When asking, "What is success, anyway?" you first have to take an honest look at yourself and then be willing to take responsibility for who you are. Once you accept responsibility, you can eliminate all the excuses you've been hiding behind.[5] How often do we tell our children, "Don't give me excuses about why you didn't do your chores or finish your homework"? Yet every day, we adults create our own excuses about why we can't get the job we want, create the financial freedom and dream life we deserve, or figure out what our passion is and go after it. Our family loves going camping and when our kids were infants and toddlers, we would just take them along with us, yet we met so many parents who stopped doing things they loved because of their children. These excuses are nothing more than stumbling blocks to your true fulfillment.

As parents, we go through life with a predefined notion of success based on society's views. We are also influenced by a standard of success that is defined by society, media, coworkers, and friends. In schools, our teachers taught us to strive for success but never gave us a true definition. Television, movies, and magazines oftentimes lead us to believe that success is measured in wealth and fame. So, to some people, success might be earning a million dollars a year while for others it might be that fancy new Corvette sitting in their garage.

R-15 or R-30 Insulation?

Anyone who has done serious remodeling will need to decide what insulation to use. Looking at the two numbers R-15 and R-30, you would think that R-30 would be best; the higher the number the better, right? Nope. You can't compare the two. Each has a different purpose. R-15 is for walls and R-30 is for the attic. The two are not interchangeable. We, too, have different purposes for our lives. There is no one else like you in the world. It is human nature to compare ourselves to each other. We mentioned earlier how television and magazines influence our definition of success.

> Let's take the example of what the media deems to be a beautiful body. Many mothers compare their bodies to the bodies they see in the media and strive to look like them. Instead, they need to embrace their bodies and realize that the majority of those women haven't given birth to beautiful, healthy children. Lose weight for personal satisfaction and to improve your health, not to look like someone else.

The primary reason you shouldn't judge your lives based on others is because there is always someone who has more money, a better car, a bigger house, or something more than what you have. But also remember, there are those who don't have as much as you, either. If you focus on how much more everyone has than you, then you are focusing on the *lack* in your life rather than the *abundance* that you already have. Inevitably, you are going to find someone who does have more than you.

> Let's say your next-door neighbors buy a new car. You see them pull out of the garage and wonder why you shouldn't have a new car, too. So you dash off and buy a new vehicle as well. The next thing you know, the couple down the street just bought an SUV. Material things don't make us happy. The problem with this is that as the newness of the latest "thing" you get wears

off, so does your excitement. You feel good for a moment, but it is only fleeting. You have to realize that you are the only one responsible for your own contentment. This is just a fact of life.

> *Our Values determine our Perception of what is right and wrong, good and bad.*

Think of how much energy and time we waste on needless comparisons. So why do we set ourselves up for failure by comparing ourselves to others? It is easier to look to the outside rather than face the fact that we have to take responsibility for our own life. The real truth is that it is more courageous to look deep inside yourself, acknowledge your weaknesses, and take the steps necessary to correct them. Those brave enough to do so meet their full potential and are successful in their own right. In addition, by doing this, they are setting an example for their children to follow as well as setting their children up for a successful future.

We are all unique in some way, which is why we shouldn't compare ourselves to others. You can't gauge your success by others. It doesn't work! Yet, most people do just that and end up putting themselves into a depressing and negative vibration. Instead of spending your time dwelling on how much money your neighbor makes or how much business your competitor has, acknowledge and embrace the qualities that make you special. Accept yourself and appreciate the special talents and qualities that you possess. Take a moment and list ten positive traits about yourself in the space on the next page.

LIST TEN POSITIVE TRAITS ABOUT YOURSELF

1. _____
2. _____
3. _____
4. _____
5. _____
6. _____
7. _____
8. _____
9. _____
10. _____

For more writing space please visit
www.ParentOutLoud.com/STEP to download your free Play-Book.

One of the primary reasons we fall into the trap of comparison is because we want approval. For some unknown reason, people feel the need to seek approval for their behavior and actions. In reality, the only opinion that really matters is your own.

This is something that we teach our kids every time they ask us if we like a drawing or project they have created. Our initial response used to be, "Of course, sweetie. I love everything you create. It's beautiful." And many would say that is a perfectly good response. Unfortunately, this reinforces the need for external approval. Now our first response is, "I'm happy to tell you what I think, but first, tell me what you think because your opinion is the only one that really matters."

This response reinforces personal satisfaction and helps develop self-esteem. The reason that the need for external approval is so detrimental is because it gives other people control over your emotions. And, with so many negative people around, this can easily cause your self-esteem to plummet.

Unless you perceive yourself as worthwhile, you cannot have high self-esteem. Our opinion of ourselves critically influences everything—from our career to our relationships to our accomplishments in life. High self-esteem leads to a happy, gratifying, and purposeful life by:

- Creating a positive attitude
- Allowing you to take responsibility
- Opening your eyes to new opportunities and challenges
- Fostering an internal drive to become better

> Self-esteem is a major component in determining what we consider to be success or failure.

So, how do we recognize poor self-esteem? Low self-esteem leads to extremes in behavior such as:

- Judging others
- Gossiping
- Feeling superior
- Acting jealous
- Seeking approval from others

Happiness and fulfillment are internal. The problem is that when you rely on external sources and they become critical or judgmental, you'll soon be brought down by them. If you're around this type of negativity, it can be detrimental. For example, if you work in an environment where the majority of the employees and management constantly gossip, it has a devastating effect on your self-esteem, especially if you're not secure in yourself. As this negativity bombards you, there is a good chance that you may start to take on that type of attitude yourself, which can lead to self-sabotaging thoughts and negative self-talk. On the other hand, if your attitude is positive, thoughts race through your head such as "I can do anything I set my mind to." The moment we transform our negativity into positive energy, our confidence and self-image skyrockets.

Minimize Negative Spaces

Small spaces are very difficult to insulate properly. Many of us own several items that take up small spaces in our homes; televisions, computers, cell phones, and portable video games. They're small, and they can be very difficult to monitor. Our kids are growing up in a world vastly different from the one we grew up in. These days, a host of social forces as well as the school systems are placing a tremendous amount of pressure on children. We live in one of the wealthiest, most technologically advanced nations on earth, yet our children suffer from chronic unhappiness, depression, and anxiety. In the past, the home was the greatest influence on children. Now, however, the media and the educational system, not the parents, have the greatest influence. At home, young kids and teenagers spend their days in front of the television, and many have one in their rooms, which means that even when the family is in the same house, its members are splintered off from each other. Children between the ages of eight to eighteen spend almost four hours a day in front of a TV screen and almost two additional hours on the computer surfing the Internet and playing video games.

The future of our country learns about life from celebrities, musicians, and the five o'clock news anchors. These messages convey that happiness stems from wealth and fame. Many of the images presented in the media, Internet, and electronic games send unrealistic messages to viewers. Yes, the actors and actresses may look beautiful and flawless, but how much of that is airbrushed or digitally altered? Some of the most detrimental aspects of the media affecting our children include:

Commercials. Did you know that approximately one out of every four commercials sends out messages that tell viewers what is or is not attractive? On average, our teens see more than 5,300 of these types of messages per year, which result in poor self-esteem and confidence issues. Advertisements along these lines inundate kids of all ages and idealizes the world to children. This distorts their version of reality.

Society often grooms us to be negative.

Violence. The average American child has seen 200,000 violent acts on television by age 18. This type of constant exposure results in the desensitization of kids and can potentially make them more aggressive. Behavior problems, nightmares, and difficulty sleeping may be a consequence of exposure to media violence.

Dangerous Behaviors. Numerous studies demonstrate that teens who watch a good deal of sexual content on television are more likely to initiate intercourse or participate in other sexual activities earlier than peers who don't watch sexually explicit shows. Many television shows depict sexual activity and substance abuse as a part of normal everyday living. Because children lack life experience, they cannot foresee the consequences of such behaviors.

Along with television, the Internet and video games wreak havoc on many children's lives. One of the primary ways is through the elimination of playtime. Children need to play in an unstructured and relaxed environment, preferably outdoors. Aside from causing obesity, the lack of play prevents the development of physical control and coordination through jumping, climbing, or even kicking a ball around. Also, children's imagination and creativity is likely to be stunted as well as their social skills. You can't make friends, learn teamwork, resolve conflict, and learn to communicate with a computer screen. Sadly, many of today's kids only know how to "play" electronically.

> Even we are affected. Long Pacific Northwest winters mean spending a lot of time indoors. We turn off the electronics and literally have to push the kids out the door when it's not raining. "But I don't want to go outside. I want to play video games! I'll be bored outside!" Within five minutes they have found something that entertains them for hours.

Some may think, "Well, it is just a television show or a video game; kids know the difference between reality and fantasy. Right?" Wrong. The negativity of the media and entertainment industry manifests itself through many behavioral problems in the education system such as random acts of violence, premarital sex, self-harm, and eating disorders. In addition to the media, the Internet, and video games, our children face additional challenges by the pressures they encounter at school such as conformity, bullying, and perfectionism.

A Continuous Barrier

A home's insulation provides a continuous barrier between inside spaces and the outside environment. As parents, we must be aware of the way outside influences can impact our family. It is our job to create a safe and loving home where our children have the freedom to express themselves. Lack of support from family members can be very difficult to handle. Have you created a situation where your children can't trust you? Have you ever shown up late when picking your child up from school? Have you ever promised your child something and then changed your mind? Does your lack of trust in others result in a negative and jaded viewpoint of the world that filters over into your son or daughter's lives? Negativity and a lack of trust sets in place harmful and destructive emotions such as jealousy, speculation, and gossip.

One negative comment has been proven to be 17 times more powerful than a positive comment.

> Motivational speaker Les Brown says, "It is important in the parental process for you to always communicate with your kids that they are special. They have greatness in them and greatness is a choice; it's not their destiny. It is the choices they make that determine whether or not they manifest greatness in their lives."

"It's an ongoing process. As parents, we don't know what's happening and what our kids' friends are saying when they are at school. Authority figures and friends are saying things to them that counteract what we say.

We have to provide *constant* positive reinforcement to our children. *One* negative comment has been proven to be 17 times more powerful than a positive comment. Give them positive

Train your mind to find out where you are and where you want to get to by striving to be the best you can.

reinforcement several times a day because faith comes by hearing, and we live in a world where you are told more about your limitations than about your potential. Parents have to be a continuous broadcasting system to overcome the constant negative news. If we say to our kids that they can't do something, someone else has to come along and say, 'You can do it, you can do it, you can do it...' 17 times to neutralize that one time."[22] Therefore, we have to constantly reinforce the positive. That's why motivational seminars, workshops, CDs, and motivational experiences are so very important to remind ourselves to override the negative conversations from our environment, peers, people we care about, and the words that are being spoken.

Negative influences that curtail our children's enthusiasm can be dealt with by the following measures:

- Talk to your children about how negativity is detrimental and look at ways to change a bad situation into a positive one. This is a great opportunity to teach about Perception and the Law of Cause and Effect.

- Give your children a strong sense of self and belief in their values. People who are not at ease with the success of others and indulge in cynicism cannot deter a child who has a firm foundation.

- Look for personal growth opportunities. You take the time to improve your life, so why not do the same for them? Personal growth isn't just for adults. Resources like books, workshops, and continuing education programs can help your children achieve confidence in the presence of overwhelming negativity. And the really cool thing is that often, your children accept concepts when they are taught by someone other than you.

- Counteract their negativity. Siblings have a tendency to want to verbally cut each other down. Refuse to accept those words in your house. Engage in activities and dialogue that promote positive feelings.

- Have an open-door policy. Children have to feel safe in order to share their feelings with you. When your child is ready to talk, they need to talk now, not when it's more convenient for you. Since your child is coming to you, they are more open to listen to your input in resolving their feelings and issues. This can halt the development of negative attitudes in the home environment.

Exceed Design Expectations

Why is character so important for parents? For starters, look at the impact your character has on your children. In the last section, we discussed the negative impact of media, video games, and the Internet, and as you may have guessed, these can be instrumental in influencing children's character. One way to help develop your children's character is to monitor their activities and interests, such as what they watch and read, and with whom they associate. Some of you reading this may think this sounds like Big Brother, but in all reality, it is our responsibility to oversee our children's activities. What type of example do you set for them?

Values are the defining factors that determine whether or not we succeed.

As speaker John Maxwell says, "Everything rises and falls on leadership." By this standard, *your* personal character becomes the character of your children. The character of a parent affects not only the behavior of their children, but their results as well. One of our primary goals must be to help our children develop positive character traits. What do we build character on? To build anything, it must have a foundation. Just as there are concrete foundations for homes and buildings, there are many foundations to build character upon. One of the best bases for character development is our value system. As parents, it can be a difficult job to instill values in your children. We can't be with our children 24/7, so we have to rely on the strength of the values we teach them. On some occasions, such as peer pressure to drink or smoke, strong values can be the difference between yes and no.

The next time that someone's actions upset you, ask yourself, "Which of my rules were broken? Why do I react the way I do?"

Values are the defining factors that determine whether or not we succeed. When you struggle or suffer, it's not what you do that counts, but whether you stay true to your values. If our actions aren't based on our values, then we experience discomfort and a lack of confidence. Living your life according to a set of strong values gives you freedom from fear and doubt because you know that you're acting according to your beliefs. There are no short cuts in life. If something seems too good to be true, ask yourself "Why?" and "Does this align with my values?"

Everything in our life relates back to values. For example, how do you decide what church is best for you and your family? Knowing your values can help you decide what type of religion is best for you. Bear in mind that your actions demonstrate what is important to you.

> If, for example, you think that one of your values is being a good parent, but you go to happy hour after work each day and spend your time at home sitting in front of your laptop, is being a good parent really a value for you? Our character needs a firm foundation, and one of the strengthening agents is values.

They are the basic building blocks, and from them, we can build and alter any character we choose to be. Values give us the power to determine the destiny of our life. Choosing our character determines the life we live. Each day we need to ask ourselves, "What character am I choosing to live" and "Am I living a value-based life?"

No Gaps

For insulation to work effectively, there can't be any gaps. For instance, if you insulate a set of stairs, the insulation has to be perfectly aligned with the stairs; otherwise, you're going to have air seep in through small gaps. In the same manner, it is important for us to pay attention to all of the messages we hear because if we don't consciously close the gap, negative words flow in. This can lead to the perpetuation of a negative attitude as well. Excitement and enthusiasm are highly important to create a fun household. Negative emotions expressed by children can be tackled through constructive dialogues. Issues should be put forth for an open discussion and inputs of the negative people should be considered.

It is extremely important as we create our lives that we pay attention to the messages we give ourselves as well as to the messages coming from outside sources. What "noise" do you have going on around you? What is the atmosphere around you? Having the news on as background noise will often create a negative, depressing atmosphere because seldom do we hear news reports that are positive and life-affirming. We hear about the horrid state of the economy, natural disasters, murders, and other sensationally negative stories. Sensationalism sells. The news is not a place to get your inspiration, and it is not information that you want going into the absorbing minds of your children who are not yet able to differentiate the good from the bad.[5] If children are learning about the world and society through television, they are getting a very skewed and depressingly negative picture.

There is a need to feel justified for having the complaints we have. We, in turn, start looking for something to fulfill us, and we keep reaching for material goods for that fulfillment. Feelings of deprivation can only come from comparing our own situation to what others tend to define as success. Reject what others define as success and look inside yourself for the answers. What makes you happy? If all of your bills were paid every month, how would you spend your days? In what activities would you partake? If it comes from the inside, then it is pure and it's yours. Train your mind to find out where you are and where you want to get to by striving to be the best you can. Values are personal and created from our emotions. Our values determine our perception of what is right and wrong, good and bad. People think that their values are right. Actually, they are neither right nor wrong except when compared to a set of rules.

> Behaviors, too, are based on rules. For example, many cultures eat with a fork and knife, while the people of India are trained to use only the tips of the fingers of the right hand to touch food. It is a major social disgrace to eat with your left hand, or to even to pick up a drinking glass with the left hand since this hand is reserved for wiping the backside after using the restroom. In other words, the right hand is the "clean" hand, while the left is the "dirty" hand.

> Another example is dining out. By finishing everything on their plate, Westerners are showing respect to the chef while the Chinese will always leave something in the middle of the table where all the food is placed. This is to show that they have more than enough, which gives respect to the host.

Who established the rules for behavior? Some come from our culture, some from our paradigms, and some from other motivators.

> We have a family member who loves dogs and has adopted several throughout her life. Sometimes, the dog's personality has not blended well with the family, so she has made the decision to find the dog another, better home. But she's met several people who have adopted dogs and are miserable living with them, yet they absolutely refuse to find the dog a new home because they are living with the belief (paradigm) that when you bring a dog into your family, it stays with you for life.

Which belief is better for the dog? Which one is better for the owner? Begin to question everything. Is this belief good for me? Is it good for my family? If it's not, create a new belief!

> *Another person's rules for values and acceptable behavior can be different than our own, and that is okay.*

Behaviors that are acceptable are often considered so because someone else defined them for us early on. Unless someone's behavior is affecting you or your space, consider carefully how much you want to stand in judgment. If you perceive the action of someone as bad and it does not directly affect you, let it go. If their action does affect you, set some boundaries to insulate yourself from those actions. Most importantly, when it comes to your own actions and your reactions to other people's actions, consider imitating the behavior of those you admire and rejecting the behaviors you see producing results you don't wish to obtain.

The next time that someone's actions upset you, ask yourself, "Which of my rules was broken? Why do I react the way I do?" And remember that everyone has their own sets of values and rules. Nothing is right or wrong; it's just different. Their values are just as important to them as yours are to you. So when you get upset, don't react; just realize that the situation just *is*. Can you just ignore the situation and be content in the knowledge that all of us are different; can you see or understand why this person might have other values and rules than you? In our world today, we have country and cultural boundaries that are dissolving, and we need to work with people on a regular basis who may have very different values and rules than our own.

When we realize that everyone has a right to their own opinion and beliefs, it opens us up to being better communicators, and we stop being so frustrated from trying to make another person conform to our rules. There is freedom in minding your own business and accepting another's differences versus tolerating them while holding a grudge or making a judgment.

Just imagine if you would only think, "Oh, they have different values and rules than me," every time something upsets you. A good exercise in awareness is to take notice when you feel really good because of something someone else said or did. What did they do that harmonized with one of your values? This increases your level of awareness, and you are able to reflect on your reactions. In doing this, you notice that you don't get so emotionally involved in what other people say or do. If you don't agree with someone, just say to yourself that they have different values and rules, and let it go. It is actually kind of fun to do this. Make a game of it, and you will find yourself changing into a happier person.

Our inner world is a reflection of our outer world. You've got to take responsibility for anything you want to change in your life. When you were young, you could blame your parents, but you've grown up. Now you're an adult. You can't continue to blame your parents. You have to take responsibility for your life. Until you do, you're not going to grow or learn. But once you start taking responsibility and acknowledging, "I've got to work on my thoughts; I've got to work on my self-esteem; I've got to work on these things," your life will dramatically change for the better in ways you can't even imagine.

Minimize Compression

People new to remodeling might think that two layers of insulation would be better than one. Actually, it has the opposite effect. Not only does it *not* double the R-Value, it actually decreases the original R-Value. For maximum effectiveness, you must let the single layer of insulation expand to its fullest capacity. Anyone who has opened a package of insulation knows that as soon as you cut the binding plastic, it explodes to three times its compressed size. Our lives are very similar. We must release our bindings and continue to constantly expand. This is a lifelong process. You grow for the rest of your life. There is no end to growing and learning. There is no end to being a student of self-development. It requires daily studying, whether it's reading a few paragraphs or pages from a book or listening to a CD in your car while driving.

Over time, we evolve, we integrate all of this learning into our lives, and we get better and better. Understand that we have infinite potential. We can be infinitely greater tomorrow than we are today. We can *never* use up all the potential that is within us. Most of us haven't even begun to tap into our potential, but there are some people who may be thinking, "I've had a good life. I've done everything I wanted to do." If this sounds familiar, you need to expand the vision of your life. Create a bigger dream! There are classes to take, children and grandchildren who need your guidance, and charities that need your help. You may not have even discovered your greatest gift yet!

"To use our potential, to move into the truth of who we are, and to achieve bigger and better goals, we must continue to grow. By studying and working on our thoughts, especially our paradigms, we can change. Through positive and uplifting messages, we move forward toward fulfilling our dreams. Once we learn to do this, we can then reach for dreams that once seemed incomprehensible. We live in a Universe with an infinite abundance of ideas. Consequently, the best way to do anything in the world has not even been thought of yet. There is always a better way when you are dealing with the infinite. So if the Universe is infinite, you can never take more than your share. There is always a bigger, better way to do something that you learned how to do yesterday. There is always a higher star to reach for. The first dream we manage to reach for is only as big as our self-esteem allows it to be.

As we grow and the belief in us grows, we can reach for a bigger dream, a bigger ideal. Then we grow and evolve. We learn some more, and we can reach for another, bigger dream. We continue to grow ... and grow ... and grow. This is how somebody like nineteenth-century American steel tycoon Andrew Carnegie could go from being a poor child to eventually becoming the first billionaire in the United States. This is how Bill Gates, who started in his garage as a college dropout, went on to create Microsoft and become a multi-billionaire. It's all because they reached for one dream, and then they reached for another. They learned to grow, believe in themselves, and keep reaching for something else. This is the real juice of life!"[30]

ACTION STEPS

1. Sit down with your family and write out a list of your values. A few examples are integrity, reliability, ethics, and honesty.

2. Turn off the TV for one week and pick one night and play games together. Don't listen to or read any news that week, and discover how that impacts you and your family.

3. Have each person in your family make a separate list of all of the positive things that you have in your life. As a family, each member writes their name on a card. Then each card is passed around and everyone writes one positive thing about the person on the card. This card is kept in a safe place to refer to when encouragement is needed.

**For more writing space please visit
www.ParentOutLoud.com/STEP to download your free PlayBook.**

CHAPTER 8

FLIPPING THE SWITCH

*Some people are always grumbling
because roses have thorns; I am thankful
that thorns have roses.*

—Alphonse Karr

"I hate piano!"

"Really, Jenny?" asked Maureen.

"I haven't practiced, and I'm going to be in such trouble. I don't ever want to do piano. I want to stop, and I hate it!" Her voice was increasing in intensity with each word.

"Oh, that's terrible! You must be feeling terrible now because you didn't do your homework, and now you are going into your lesson unprepared. I can really understand the way you are feeling."

Maureen could see her daughter's body start to relax.

"But what am I going to do?" said Jenny.

"Well, if I were in your shoes, I would go to my lesson and do my very best. I would take responsibility for my choices and learn from them. Did you learn something here?"

Jenny smiled. "Yes, I learned to make sure I practice every day before I go out to play."

"Do you need my help to remember?" said Maureen.

"Nope; I got it, Mom."

Knowing that her daughter feels heard and validated, Maureen scoops up her keys. "Let's go. I think you're going to be surprised how well you play for your teacher."[25]

Where's The Power?

Many people transform their lives by starting with a change in attitude. Initially, they feel unsure of themselves, but after changing their thought process, eliminating the negative, and focusing on their good qualities, they form a new confident self-esteem. The reason this approach works is because *if* you believe you are great ... *then* you are great! Remember: you are unique. You must have this belief in yourself to accomplish your life's dreams. Once you develop and maintain a strong sense of self and a positive attitude, you create the experiences that support this belief. A good illustration of this point is a job interview. If you enter the interview with a meek and timid approach, you've given them the impression that you may not be able to handle the responsibilities of the job. Your body language gives you away faster than your words. Your flimsy handshake, lack of eye contact, and meek tone of voice are signals that tell a prospective employer within seconds whether or not you are able to handle the job. However, if you go in prepared and confident, asking all of the right questions as well as making sure that the job is a good fit for you too, you give the prospective employer a completely different impression about your capabilities.

Attitude is a composite of your thoughts, feelings, and results. All you need to do with children to help them change their attitude is to tweak just one little part of their thoughts. **Our thoughts create our feelings. Our feelings create our actions. And our actions create our results.**[5]

Installing Hard Wiring

When we first came into the world, our needs could be counted on one hand: food, comfort, physical contact, and sleep. But by the time we reach adulthood, our little baby list of needs has ballooned to a list several pages long. How does this happen? When we are children, our brains are rapidly developing, with millions of neural connections being made and then used repeatedly until they become mental habits that we carry into adulthood. Huge amounts of data, mostly from adult sources, stream into developing brains. Children come into this world devoid of any beliefs, like an empty cup. Input from parents fills that cup over the years. Much of it is good information, like, "It's a good idea to wear a coat when it's snowing," "This is how we cook a meal," and "It's not safe to drive a car after drinking alcohol." Unfortunately, adults pass on bad information as well.[5] Children aren't mature enough to separate the good from the bad, so they also believe and internalize much of the bad. For example:

> **Attitude is a composite of your thoughts and your feelings and your results. All you need to do with a child to help them change their attitude is to tweak just one little part of their thoughts.**

"You're not worthy!"

"Why aren't you as smart as the other kids in your class?"

"We can't afford it."

"A job provides financial security."

For many of us, when we grow up, our little voice takes over the negative data input job that was once the province of the adults in our lives. The chaff we internalized as youngsters hardens into the core beliefs we have about ourselves as adults. This colors not only our own internal dialogue (i.e., the monkey chatter constantly talking in your head), but also the way we perceive and interact with others. We also are living with the bad mental habits of our parents, teachers, aunts, uncles, and friends. For instance, the lengthy roster of "needs" we've accumulated primarily consists of mere wants and desires. We know that, intellectually, if we take the time to think about it.

> A great illustration is TV. No one actually needs a TV for survival, but we probably all know someone who, if pressed to cancel their cable subscription, would say they couldn't live without their soaps, football, or 24-hour news. We watch very little television. Initially, we thought we'd miss it, but the tradeoff between the *wasted* time spent staring at a box was tenfold to the *quality* time we gained with our kids and creating our family's financial independence. We learned how much they have to offer this world and are constantly amazed at how creative and smart they are.

The Universe is unlimited, and anything we want is ours for the taking. But this can only happen when we actually believe this is true.

Parents are the most influential force in their children's lives. Our children pick up who we are as people, not only by what we say, but even more by the actions we take, and the thoughts we think, in the strongest and most significant ways. We can't hide who and what we really are from our children. They are so smart! They know when you say one thing and do the exact opposite. Realizing this link in the importance of our physical, emotional, spiritual, and mental well-being is imperative for our children's well being and attitude.

To build your self-esteem, you must overcome any fears, anxieties, self-doubts, and limiting beliefs that you may have, such as, "I can't do it," or "I'm not good enough." The best method to do this is to focus on your unlimited potential. Know that you can do anything you want when you set your mind to it and believe. With repetition and practice, this process reverses those fears and anxieties and builds the self-esteem you need to meet the challenges you face. You find yourself succeeding more and more, and you feel good.

> We often find our children saying, "I can't." We have different responses to this based on the child's age. In response to our three-year old, we'll say, "Well, that's stinkin' thinkin'!" to which he replies, "Yep, I'm stinkin' and I'm thinkin'." Whereas, when our older children say, "I can't," we respond with, "If you tell yourself you can't, then you're right. You need to tell your brain that you *can* and it will make you right."

The keys to self-esteem include:

- Visualizing yourself as a success
- Creating an awareness of your talents, qualities, and accomplishments
- Affirming you are a successful person who has the ability to accomplish your goals

Whenever we think about what we do well, it's a form of self-affirmation that builds self-esteem and reinforces our positive beliefs. But sometimes we forget about our good qualities and talents. To counteract such anxieties about ourselves, we need to remind ourselves of who we are and what we are capable of doing, so that we can have what we want. When was the last time you paid attention to your inner world and listened to your positive inner voice? As you pay attention to your inner self, your insight awakens. You are able to become conscious of what infuses your external world. At various times during our lives, we experience challenges and stressful situations. No one is exempt from these events. Life isn't perfect. Life happens. The world we live in today is full of crime, disorder, and negativity, and many of us have lost sight of what true fulfillment is. Why is it that so many of us walk around as if we are carrying the weight of the world on our shoulders? Do you look upon every adversity you face as life ending?

LIST TEN THINGS THAT YOU DO WELL

1. _____
2. _____
3. _____
4. _____
5. _____
6. _____
7. _____
8. _____
9. _____
10. _____

**For more writing space please visit
www.ParentOutLoud.com/STEP to download your free Play-Book.**

Plug into Your Surge Protector

Children learn by example and experience. When our children see us remain calm, we teach them by modeling the behavior. We can also teach our children the science behind how our brains learn through the Six Intellectual Faculties. So much starts to make sense when we understand this. You are constantly training your brain, and it's the job of a parent to train a small child's brain, too. Stop and think about the magnitude of this responsibility.

> "When our children have tantrums, we don't try to stop them. They have the tantrum but in a 'time-out zone.' We support them by using a very loving, slow, and empathetic tone, 'I know.' Pause. 'You can do as much screaming as you want. When you are done and you can talk and make your voice as quiet as mine, then you can come back and be with us.'"[21]

When parents learn to stop and reflect rather than react, their stress lifts because they're using their Intellectual Faculties.

> We often don't give ourselves sufficient credit for all we've accomplished, particularly when we encounter difficulties in life.

In the previous chapters, we discussed the importance of a positive, healthy mindset. People who have a healthy self-image realize their strengths but accept their faults and weaknesses as well. The same is true with regard to the integration of your attitude into your life. It is imperative to shift your outlook from one of negativity to a constructive and encouraging attitude. This may come as a surprise, but your attitude is more important than your aptitude in determining your success in life. You can learn to have an optimistic outlook on life, but it needs to be purposefully installed into your daily living routine. If you are bothered with persistent negative thoughts, you can replace this mindset with a new positive attitude. And wouldn't it be great to instill this kind of attitude into your children?

Where to Focus the Light

Let's take a look at a real-life example of choosing your focus. "You talk to a child, who struggles with math and English but is doing really well in spelling. The child brings home the report card, and none of the grades are very good except for one. There was one decent grade; even if it's not an A, it's a B, which is better than all the rest.

The parent's natural reaction is to say; 'You need to bring up your math grade, and you got an F on this" and on and on ...' You talk about all the bad grades. You never talk about the one thing the child did right. Consequently, the attitude of the child is not going to change because you're asking for improvement to something that is a weakness. Who wants to spend time doing that? You want to help intensify strengths.

What would happen if you only looked at the good grade in spelling and praised the child by saying, 'Look at that! You got a B in spelling! That is so awesome!' You don't talk about the things that were bad. You talk about the *one* that was good. That inspires the child and creates desire to get two or three good grades in addition to the grade in spelling.

When you talk about the one good thing your children did, your children believe in themselves more. If you talk about the bad grades, their belief in themselves plummets and their self-esteem starts drowning, 'Oh, I can't get good grades; I'm a bad student.' Instantly, you have helped them create a *negative* belief and the grades will never go up.

But if you talk about only the good grade and provide praise, they are going to feel good about themselves. 'Wow! I did great in spelling!' They are going to think to themselves at some point, 'I wonder if I could do the same thing with math? If I can do it for spelling, I bet I can do it for math because I like math.' Do you see how powerful positive dialogue is?

These are the thoughts that will go through your children's heads. They will try harder because they want more of your praise! They aren't going to be satisfied with that one little bit; they want more. In addition, if your children bring up the subject in discussion, you have a perfect teaching moment: 'You know, honey, you can decide what you want for a math grade. If you want a B in math next semester, all you have to do is see it. Feel how happy you would be to earn a B in math. You know what it feels like to have a B in spelling. What would it feel like to have B in math?'"[30]

Our thoughts create our feelings. Our feelings create our actions. And our actions create our results.

Children have different personalities, and they learn in different ways. You've just got to be patient with them. "Teach your children that it is okay to fail, that every Master was once a disaster. Children need to learn that everyone makes mistakes. Mistakes are your feedback from the Universe that a change in direction is required. Everyone starts off at the bottom and was born ignorant. The purpose of your life is to get a good education and do what you love. You need to recognize opportunity and take action because at the end of the day, the Universe rewards action. It doesn't matter about how many times you fail. What matters is how many times you get back up and try again."[27]

Is Your Circuit Breaker Overloaded?

Examine your attitude toward yourself, career, relationships, and life in general. Would you rate the altitude of your attitude as soaring high, under the radar, or grounded? Where would you be if you raised your attitude vibration higher? Improve your outlook, and you soon view your life from a new perspective. Rather than focusing on what is not working or what you don't want, focus on what *is* working and what you *do* want.[5] Have you ever noticed that as you focus on how much your children are bickering, they just seem to keep doing it more? As your perspective improves, your self worth and esteem strengthens. The more positive your attitude, the more self-confident and together you feel, and your children notice it as well. They become more confident and respect your opinion more because you speak from a position of strength. You will be amazed at the difference this makes in your overall life.

> We often don't give ourselves sufficient credit for all we've accomplished, particularly when we encounter difficulties in life.

Are you an eternal pessimist? This thought process can be a vacuum. Once you begin to feel this way, you're sucked into a constant stream of negative thoughts. How do we pull ourselves out of this pit? We need to tap back into a positive attitude that we've lost somewhere in life. Just as proper nutrition and exercise fuels our physical bodies, our attitude is the energy that propels our wants and desires into manifestation. The same is true for our children.

To change your paradigm is similar to when children first learn to walk. They had to continue to stumble and fall until they were able to put one foot in front of the other, walk out the door, and take advantage of the opportunities that awaited them. As parents, we did not tell them to give it up when they took one step and fell down. Instead, we cheered, applauded, smiled, and told them how great they were for taking that one step! Unfortunately, as we get older, our limiting beliefs begin to create expectations and models of how things ought to be, how others should behave, and even how they should think and how the world should treat us. This inner paradigm encompasses all of our life: my new gel-point roller pen, my parking space, my chair, my spouse, my self-image, and my prestige too. As you rid your mind of more of these defeating patterns, you'll be able to spend more time seeing clearly and living the life you deserve! One technique that we learned from Byron Katie, author of *Loving What Is*, is to question everything with "Is it true?" You will be astounded at how many things in your life really aren't true.

A negative attitude about ourselves, our relationships, or our career keeps us grounded. If you want your life to soar to new heights then you need to *raise the altitude* of your attitude. The following questions will help you determine the elevation of your attitude.

- How do you feel about your job? Do you love going to work each morning? Or do you dread Sunday nights because you know Monday is just around the corner? Did you know that more heart attacks happen on Mondays than any other day of the week?

- How are the relationships in your life? Are you enthusiastic when you spend time with those around you? Or does the energy seem to drain out of the room as soon as you walk in?

- How do you feel about yourself? Do you think you have true value and worth to offer?

We have the power to flip our own switch and choose the altitude of our attitude. Allowing our attitude to remain stuck at ground level creates a lot of tension and strain. Choosing to raise our attitude allows us, and those around us, to grow and flourish. Take a moment and think about this: how would your world be affected if you had a positive and upbeat attitude? What if you were to face life more enthusiastically and deal more effectively with inevitable problems? Not only does our attitude affect our behavior, it also affects our perceptions. When the altitude of your attitude is ground level, your vision is restricted, and you can only see what is right in front of you. For instance, how would you react if someone scratched your car? Would you be upset or just accept it and move on? Raising your attitude gives you a whole new perspective, one where you are hovering in the clouds looking down at the smallness of your problems, one that allows you to view what you previously considered challenges and obstacles and to now view them as new and exciting opportunities.

Complete the Circuit

For parents, or anyone for that matter, learning to release the past is like the difference between night and day.

> Before we became parents, we were not as forgiving and instead were very judgmental. We would look at a child who behaved poorly and blame the behavior on the parents. With the ability to let go, we learned to embrace whatever came. Now, it's funny: people say to us all the time, "There is such a difference in you two! We don't mean to hurt your feelings, but before, you would complain about your kids, how they were giving you grief, and you didn't know what to do. Now, you just take life in stride. I've never met a stronger or more grounded couple. And your children are so well behaved." This is a joy to hear since our children are not so well behaved at home. This means we are at peace, have a sense of calm, and have created a safe, loving home. Our children have picked up on that.

When you have peace as a parent, that changes everything. Before, life was so chaotic and it was "Poor me; I'm not sure how much more of this I can take!" We were stuck in victim mode. We've now learned that life happens and it can get in the way of so many things if you choose to let it. Before, we didn't want to follow our dreams. Instead, we chose to hold onto past mistakes and failures. Now, nothing gets in our way; we've not only succeeded but taught our children perseverance as well.

Reset the Circuit Breaker

When you have six items using the same outlet and drawing too much power, the circuit becomes overloaded, which trips the circuit breaker and stops the flow of electricity. Having resentment toward another stops the flow of energy through your body. Forgiveness is your own personal reset button to your circuit breaker. Are you still letting the things you have done in the past and the things others have done, influence your life now? One of the best illustrations we have heard is that refusing to forgive someone is like taking poison and expecting the other person to die. The people who have hurt you are not spending any time thinking about the situation or event. They probably wouldn't even remember whatever happened, if you asked them. But *you* relive it over and over again. You keep an open wound inside of you and poison your own life.[5]

Forgiveness is not about the other person. It is for you. Author Catherine Ponder states, "When you hold resentment toward another, you are bound to that person or condition by an emotional link that is stronger than steel. Forgiveness is the only way to dissolve that link and get free." Forgiveness is easy once you stop dwelling on the injustices or perceived injustices done to you by someone else. As these negative thoughts invade your mind, practice replacing them with good thoughts instead. In doing this you'll soon find that these unforgiving thoughts rarely come into your conscious thoughts and become "no big deal." Then, true forgiveness occurs naturally. Soon, you can see your unforgiving thoughts as a silly part of your past or, even better, a lesson from which you grew and overcame pettiness or resentment.

The art of forgiveness gives us a possibility to grow and foster a positive attitude. When we let go of our resentments, we heal and become better human beings. This is a great step for living with an optimistic outlook. By letting go, you heal the wound. Often, it is things *we* have done that cause us the most pain. People we've hurt, bad choices we've made, or just negative thoughts we've held about ourselves and others only serve to sabotage our lives and the results we get. Often, when we make big, bold decisions to move toward our dreams, the little voice in our head reminds us of all the times we failed, and we jump back into safety. We revert to blaming someone else, a situation, or even worse, ourselves! So it becomes even more important to forgive ourselves. Stop playing the "blame-game." Forgive and move forward.

It was absolutely liberating for us when we realized that all of the events that have happened in our lives, both the good and bad, have brought us to the place we are today. And by forgiving ourselves for past actions, we freed up so much space and energy for the goals we wanted to achieve. Be grateful for your experiences, learn from them, and move forward with increased knowledge, especially the knowledge that forgiveness matters and can be a wonderful tool for moving forward. When we forgive, the Universe opens up new, more profound and loving experiences.

We once heard someone say that you repeat the bad things in your life until you have learned from them. Only then are you ready to move forward. Ralph Waldo Emerson said, "Every soul has to learn the whole lesson for itself." We truly believe this.

We discovered a perfect example during our interview with Stephen M. R. Covey. When questioned about whether there was anything he wished his parents had done differently, he couldn't find one thing. But when he became a parent, he often revisited his father's chapter on Active Listening from *The 7 Habits of Highly Effective People.* He grew up immersed in his parent's techniques, but still had to do his own personal growth in learning how to relate better to his children.

Question everything with "Is it true?" You will be astounded with how many things in your life really aren't true.

Have you ever noticed that often you get similar situations or reactions occurring all at once in your life? Maybe you have conflicts with friends or coworkers where it seems everyone is against you. Take the time when this occurs to see what your role is in it and what lesson needs to be learned. Are you failing to forgive or simply blaming others for the apparent chaos? Your energy is getting sucked up in all of the drama, and often we let it drag us further into the destruction versus seeing what we can do to take responsibility and resolve the issues and conflict. It can often be as simple as saying "I was wrong. I am sorry."

Replace the Wiring

When we live in opposition to what makes us happy and fulfilled, our emotions are in turmoil, and our mind is bombarded with obsessive thoughts. Our goals, happiness, and even our health can become compromised. It is important to create balance in your life by demolishing any aspect of a negative attitude and rebuilding a newer, stronger, more hope-filled life. You may be saying to yourself that this sounds good, but it will be difficult to do. The truth is that it's not hard at all; the basic truths revealed in this book are applicable to everything, to all possible life experiences.

"A book can be a great mentor, but we also personally subscribe to the teachings of several mentors. We make every attempt to surround ourselves with like-minded individuals. When you surround yourself with the presence and experience of successful, positive-minded teachers and mentors who know what works because they have studied it for years, and now study their readings and teachings, that inherently rubs off on us as parents. We then, in turn, can share our knowledge with our children.

Ask your children, 'What is the power of our mind?' Teach them the answer, 'You become what you think about.' A two-year-old can learn it. It's amazing! Another one is 'Never be good when you can be great.' Imagine what this creates in your children's magnificent minds. It is just as easy to dream big as it is to dream small, so why dream small?"[9]

> One of our mentors, Bob Proctor, has studied belief systems for almost 50 years. At the age of 26, Bob was a firefighter in Canada earning $4,000 a year. The problem was that he owed $6,000. He had two months of high school education and a bad attitude, with a capital "A." He knew something had to change. It wasn't until someone handed him a copy of *Think and Grow Rich* by Napoleon Hill that his life started to improve. In one year, his income skyrocketed to over $175,000, and in another year, he was earning over a million dollars.

You may be thinking to yourself, "All this from a book?" Yes, it is true. What Bob learned in that book helped him to create a paradigm shift.[5] As you learned earlier, a paradigm is nothing more than a set of beliefs, often inherited from your parents or grandparents. Although those beliefs were taught to us with the best intentions, with later analysis, we find that often those beliefs are destructive and false. Remember the story about the child with the B in spelling?

For Bob, it wasn't enough that he had made a huge amount of money. He wanted to know why this was happening. He didn't feel like he had done anything particularly special, but something he was doing was significantly different from his firefighting peers. Bob was raised with the idea (paradigm) that if you were rich, you had to have a formal education and be intelligent. So he set out to study his own beliefs and realized that the lens he was viewing life through wasn't his own. Just like us, he had been living according to a preconceived set of ideas.[5]

Bob taught us that our brains are an electronic switching station, and we can activate our brain cells and cause a change in our vibration. We find this to be amazing, which is why we want to share this information with you. Once this change occurs, you can change your life and attract what you desire. One of the most influential movies we've seen based on this concept is *The Secret*. As a matter of fact, the phenomenal success of this movie and its concepts has launched a follow up movie, *Beyond the Secret*, which takes the concepts to a whole new level.[5]

After reading this, you now realize that many of our emotions, likes and dislikes, and especially our cherished belief systems with which we identify so deeply are *not* who we really are. Author Napoleon Hill says that the difference between winners and losers is the ability to make fast decisions. People with a lot of problems can't make good, sound decisions in a relatively quick manner. Take a look at how you are living. What do you see? Do you like what you see? Your answer is an expression of your paradigms. Everything you would like to alter is a reflection of a paradigm that needs to change. Do you like your finances, or do you have an inherited belief holding you back? Perhaps you think that money doesn't grow on trees or that you don't have what it takes to start a business.

Do you like your relationship with your spouse? Perhaps you think that conflict is a natural part of a loving relationship. What about your relationship with your children? Do you believe that children should be seen but not heard? Should they obey their parents? Is the parent the one who is always right? One night our 11-year-old daughter actually had the personal fortitude to tell us that we were wrong on whether our discussion was about the Law of Attraction or the Law of Cause & Effect. As we thought about the situation, it became more evident that Justine had stronger evidence for Attraction than we had for Cause & Effect, and we changed our opinion. How amazing is that? Give your children the opportunity to use their Reasoning power to change *your* mind.

> **The more personal growth you do as an individual, the happier you are, the more fulfilled you feel, the better your life works. You are a happier person to be around. Your kids feel that.**

"One of the things we've noticed is that investing in ourselves produces the best returns. There is no 401K, real estate property, or other investment that has ever produced nearly as good a return as investing in our children and ourselves. For us to truly become happy, we always have to be progressing. Not understanding who you are and what you want in life is often what keeps us from progressing."[7]

"Are you a parent who lives a life just going through the motions? Are you living a life of mediocrity where you just mark off the milestones? Went to college ... Check. Got married ... Check. Got my job ... Check. Retired ... Check. Died ... Check."[7] Who wants to live that way when you can follow your dreams and watch your children do the same? There will always be challenges, no matter what kind of life you live, but instead of letting the external world be in control of your life, you can definitely live the life that *you* control.

That's where education, knowledge, progression, and power have the greatest impact. The only thing we can master in this life is ourselves. We can't control the decisions of people around us. Yes, we may be able to influence and persuade others, but that will only take us so far. All we can control is ourselves.

"Like it says in the New Testament, 'The truth will set you free.' Finding your truth is how you can experience a fuller life and feel greater peace of mind. You need to learn how to do that. You need to learn to create deeper relationships, be able to truly have a positive impact on society, and be able to feel like you add value. To do that, you need to grow and progress. We can't define the truth that will make our life much more enjoyable by just sitting in front of the TV and hoping for our life to change because somebody else is going to change it for us. That's not how it works."[7] One of the byproducts of personal growth is that the more you do as an individual, the *happier* you are, the more *fulfilled* you feel, and the *better* your life works. You are a happier person to be around. Your kids feel that. As parents, you teach your children by the way you live your life.

Our children now see us read, listen to motivational CDs, and attend workshops and seminars. We don't watch much television. Not because we're against television but it's just that very little programming leaves us feeling happy and motivated. We used to love all of the popular crime series television programs because they are extremely well-written mysteries. Analysis of what we were absorbing revealed a string of three to six murders every week with gruesome visuals. Not too uplifting. Our children now see the investment of our time and finances of our own continual growth is an important endeavor, and it is rubbing off on them.

The Energy Is Flowing

Get some new routines into your life. Take notice of where your energy flows. You can swim with the flow of the river of life or try to paddle upstream against the current. This latter choice is exhausting and leaves you spent and useless! After a while, you learn to listen to your energy level. If things you do make you feel like your energy is sucked out of you, then whatever it is you are doing is not right. It is not in harmony with creating the life you want. Your fortune and your bliss come when you are aligned with your purpose and follow the flow. Reaching your goal is not about "getting." It is about "allowing" the energy to flow to you and through you, which, in effect, supports you on your journey. As strange as it may sound, working diligently on something you love actually gives you an abundance of energy. You'll have trouble going to sleep at night, and you'll be so excited to get going every morning.

> **We all have talents, gifts, and uniqueness. Our obligation is to accept these gifts and spend our lives sharing our gifts with our children.**

We only have one life, and none of us know if it's going to be short or long. Make sure you make the most of what you are given. We all have talents, gifts, and uniqueness. Our obligation is to accept these gifts and spend our lives sharing our gifts with our children. What are your talents? What gives you flow? How can you serve? We are here to serve—not to deserve. What value are you contributing to society? Doing what you love and focusing on how you can create value brings wealth and prosperity. When you come from a place of growth and abundance, you celebrate the success of others. Their achievements do not take way from your success. Competition comes from a belief that there is not enough, and that belief instills negativity. Competition demands that in order for me to get what I want, I must take it from someone else. Just imagine how different your life would be if you came from a platform of abundance and believed that there was more than enough for everyone. What would the future hold for our children? Some of the greatest accomplishments come from people working together to create a win-win situation. Help other people to succeed and reach their goals. Wish only the best for others, and you'll be blessed with abundance.

Remember, a person's attitude is often more important than their skill set. The way they view the world and handle challenges definitely impacts their entire life. For example, children who complain all the time about not being very good in school, how tough the assignments are, and how much the teacher doesn't like them are going to have a much tougher time than those who are proactive about solving problems and dedicated to doing the best job they can.

ACTION STEPS

If you have a persistent feeling of dullness, fatigue, sadness, and free-floating anxiety or "the blahs," look at your current attitude. If your attitude needs a makeover, the following exercise can help you determine the culprits.

- Write down all of your **negative** thoughts that come to mind most easily and look at them as a whole.

- Next to each adverse thought, write down a way to make it a **positive** thought. This is most easily done by writing the exact opposite of the negative thought. For example: "I am not smart enough to run my own business" can be changed to, "I am smart enough to run my own multimillion dollar company."

Once you've created your list, you can see how easy it is to turn a negative thought into a positive one. Keep in mind that when you first begin this Action Step, you may feel like you're not telling the truth, but through repetition (remember the NASA study), you'll be able to turn your internal dialogue around. Carry your list around with you, and every time you have a negative thought, pull out your list and read the positive thoughts you wrote about yourself. This places you in the right frame of mind to transform your current thought into an encouraging one.

For more writing space please visit
www.ParentOutLoud.com/STEP to download your free PlayBook.

CHAPTER 9

THE FINAL INSPECTION

You've got to be careful if you don't know where you're going, because you might not get there.

–Yogi Berra

"Dad, I'm thinking of quitting the swim team."

"Well, Arthur, I don't know. I don't swim and I'm not on the swim team. Why are you quitting?" Brad asked.

"Well, I've been thinking about it. When I leave high school, swimming isn't going to be a part of my career, so it isn't going to make any difference."

Brad was thoughtful. "That's true. I don't know anyone who earns money swimming."

"Do you think it's okay?"

"I don't know. I'm not on the team. You are a strong member of the team, and the coach likes you. Are you committed to the team?" he asked, admiring his son, who was growing to be taller than he was himself.

"Well, yeah."

"Do you think it's okay to quit?" Brad asked.

"I think it's okay." Arthur said.

"If you think it's okay, it's okay. Then quit. You've got to make that decision, not me."

Arthur pushed back his stool and started to walk away. "Before you go, Arthur, there is something you want to consider. Getting up at four o'clock and going to swim isn't easy, is it?"

"No, it's not."

"That could be part of the determining factor here." Brad said, "You are having trouble with this, and you are struggling with it, aren't you?"

"Yeah." Arthur replied a little sheepishly.

Brad continued, "You are probably having trouble going to tell the coach you are quitting, aren't you?"

"Yeah."

"So, what happens next time when you want to quit something you've committed to; will it be easier or harder to quit?"

"Easier," Arthur said.

"Which kind of person do you want to be?" Brad said, "It's up to you; you make your own decisions."

Do you think Arthur quit the swim team? Of course he didn't. Did you notice that Brad only asked questions? Brad views parenting a lot like selling. You answer the question with a question. You are selling them on the idea of making their own decisions. Most people don't want to do that. They are afraid their children will make a decision and it will be the wrong one. But in reality, it seems to be the wrong decision because it is the one *you* don't want them to make. *Kids are an extension of you. You programmed them.* If they go in the wrong direction, it's because you steered them in the wrong direction. So, how many decisions do you make for your children every day?[5]

Who's In Charge?

> Imagine that you have spent 12 months looking for a new home for your family. You have finally found the perfect dwelling, and from your inspection, everything looks good. The house is a little more than you budgeted, but the kids are so excited that they've already chosen their rooms. You are ready to sign the four pounds of paperwork. But wait; there is one more *decision* to make. Do you hire a home inspector? It's not required. Do you pay more money for the inspection or take your chances? The house looks fine, right? Should you spend $500 to have someone tell you this house is perfect or save the $500 and take the chance that you won't have to spend $15,000 for termite damage or $30,000 for a new roof? The decision looks a little easier now, doesn't it?

We have learned that everything happens in our lives because of the *decisions*, or *lack of decisions*, we make every day.[5] So many of us say to ourselves, "I wish we had more money; I want a new car; I'd like to lose 30 pounds; wouldn't it be nice to take a vacation to Hawaii." Not one of these will happen because they aren't decisions. Nothing will be attracted into your life until you *decide* that it will happen. The great thing is that you've already done this several times in your life. Remember when you *decided* to get a job? You didn't know how you were going to get a job, and you didn't know what company would choose you. You looked in the newspaper, talked to everyone you knew, filled out numerous applications and didn't quit until you secured the job. How could you? You needed to feed and shelter yourself. All you need to do is apply this power to everything else you want in your life, no matter how big.

So, how many times do you make decisions for your children?

> Our kids are starting to understand that we just don't dialogue like we used to. Every time they ask us something we say, "Well, what do you think you should do?"
>
> Our daughter will retort, "Stop that. Don't do that to me."
>
> "What do you think is right?
>
> You see, they know what is right and wrong; they just do.

Children are going to pick up what you teach them. And if they truly don't know, it becomes a perfect opportunity to show them all the choices that you know. Remember how Bob Proctor quoted Albert Schweitzer in our Foreword? "Example is not the main thing in influencing others; it is the only thing." Albert Schweitzer was a pretty brilliant guy, and we think he is right. You've got to set an example for your kids. You've got to make your own decisions. You've got to be decisive and live the way you want to live, and they will pick it up. If you are not living the life you desire, they will pick that up and recreate it.

Peace of mind comes from making decisions and living your path. Author Leslie Householder shared this story:

> Money was tight, but it was our anniversary, and we decided, that instead of being in fear, we were just going to go celebrate all these years together at our favorite restaurant. We would spend the money and we would face tomorrow when it came. We went with this attitude of enthusiasm and expectation over our future and knowing that we were serving people with what

we do. We had a wonderful time, and as we finished dinner, we paid the bill, and then we left. We were out in the parking lot; the waiter came running after us with paper in his hand. He gave us our receipt back and said, "The manager said that because it was your anniversary the meal is on us." We just looked at each other and we grinned. We *knew* we were doing the right thing by following our dreams. I am convinced that it is because God has something for us all to do, and our dreams are put in our hearts for a reason. When we trust that and follow it, He supports it.

> **When your parents don't believe in you, then you start not believing in you. When your parents don't tell you, "I love you," that hurts the self-esteem of the child. A lot of children don't grow up with hugs.**

The greatest changes in our lives have been results because of our dedication to improve ourselves. A few years ago, we decided that we had to invest in our own dreams. As parents, when you love your kids so much, it's almost a natural thing for you to put all your efforts and time into their needs. There are baseball uniforms, color guard, piano lessons, play dates with friends, vacations, and birthday parties. But how much do those activities really help your kids? We have seen massive changes in our kids and ourselves because of the self-improvement workshops and seminars we have attended. The best example is our success/dream journal. One day, out of the blue, our son came in, showed us his journal, and thanked us for teaching him to go for his dreams, too. That is huge!

Check the Sound System

"Many people believe that children should be seen and not heard, and they don't listen to their children. When you grow up undervalued, it takes a toll on your self-esteem. When your parents don't believe in you, then you start not believing in you. When your parents don't tell you, 'I love you,' that hurts the self-esteem of the child. A lot of children don't grow up without hugs."[30] This is one of the reasons we wrote this book. We want to help parents give their children the best foundation possible. Not only do we teach our children, but we also learn from them every day. We also appreciate our own parents even more because we understand how hard we work and realize our parents have done the same for us. Once the tables turn, you truly value your parents. "We've also learned one of the most important aspects of our relationship with our children is the power of listening. This is so overlooked. We are so anxious to give our kids advice and our motive is good. We try to protect them from making mistakes or repeating our personal mistakes, so we are anxious to give them advice.

The importance of truly *understanding* your child's feelings first before giving the advice makes such a difference. If you go to the advice first before they feel understood, they are still fighting for understanding, they are still fighting for that acceptance, and they don't want your advice yet. They won't be able to hear it. This is a conscious choice a parent has to make every day."[34]

> Even while writing this book, it was so easy to have a child chattering over our shoulder while we typed away mumbling, "Uh-huh" in the appropriate places. *Stop* what you're doing for 60 seconds and give your child your full attention. Look them in the eyes; paraphrase what they said: "So let's see if I understand this ... Wow, you must feel really frustrated. I think I would feel that way too. Would you like me to help you work through it or would you like my advice?" Only after talking and feeling understood will they be ready to hear your wisdom.

Setting a positive example for your children always comes first. It is still the most effective teacher. After you set a good example, you can focus on building a strong relationship based on trust.

Remember, you have to practice what you preach. Once you've acted accordingly and developed a bond, you can teach them how to be successful in life. If you skip either of the first two steps, listening and understanding, then they won't listen to you because you come across preachy and self-righteous. Your influence with them will be far less. But if you seek to understand them first, you'll have a much greater influence on them. Just for clarification, understanding doesn't mean agreeing with them. In a healthy relationship, disagreements are okay and can be easily solved. Every interaction like this builds and strengthens the trust bond between you and your child. And trust is critical to maintain a happy and safe home.

Checking Details

We spend so much time and energy mostly seeing the behavior that they are not doing correctly that we miss all the small opportunities to notice what they do right. We think we have to acknowledge the bigger accomplishments they do, but even if you just acknowledge those small things on a daily basis, you are going to get a whole different response from your children. Our friend Deena Morton shared this moving story:

> "I was really struggling when my son moved out two years earlier than we planned. I remember calling Bob Proctor.
>
> "Bob, what do I do about this?"
>
> "You want to control him," he said after listening to the circumstance.
>
> I said, "No I don't."
>
> "Yes you do."
>
> "No, I don't," and I really felt like I didn't.
>
> He said, "Yes, you do."

"Well, tell me why. Why do you think I want to control him?" Deena said,

"Because you think you know what's best. *That is **not** your decision. You think you know what is best for him and **that** is controlling someone.*"

I thought, Whoa! Because from my view, it didn't look like I was controlling.

He said, "You may know what is best for him, but he needs to figure that out on his own. Allow him to make his own decision. Just let go."

"Okay, I will," and she did. It was that easy.

Deena's experience taught us that "thinking you know what is best for your child" is controlling them. This type of thought process is based on your own life experiences, not your children's. As parents, we need to work on being more of a mentor or a guide, so we are someone they come to because they respect our input. They don't feel like we're pushing our opinion on them or being forthright with what we think. We are transitioning from having our children be dependent on us to becoming productive individuals who can make their own decisions.

Faulty Building Code

We were very fortunate and wise to realize shortly after the birth of our first child that there may be something indeed holding us back. It was liberating to learn that our issues were easily corrected by reevaluating our belief systems. This wasn't an easy process, but it was worth every ounce of work we put in. Parents who truly love their children are willing to do whatever it takes to give them a better life. We work hard at succeeding in our jobs, giving our children a nice home, and providing them with food. But for some, it is much easier to only focus on giving them the tangibles in life. We're willing to do whatever is necessary for the externals, but in most cases, we don't spend too much energy on providing the best internal environment for our children. Take, for example, the way you speak to your children. "Do you quickly go from quiet to yelling with nothing in between? Many of us grew up with parents like this, and there are still remnants of it today in our lives. Let's look at why it is so difficult to change.

When your children are very young, like the ones and the twos, their natural instinct is to explore. They are the ultimate explorers. They want to see, feel, listen, touch, taste, smell, and climb. They get into everything because that is what they are supposed to do. The parent gets overly protective and yells at them, 'No, don't touch that! Don't do this! Don't grab that! Put that back!' It's no, no, no, no, no!

Finally, as children get a little older, they become afraid to explore and afraid to touch. The child's little voice is screaming at them, 'I can't do this and I can't do that. I don't want to make Mommy mad so I can't do it.' Not only that, a lot of parents make their love conditional. 'If you don't stop that, you are going to get it! If you don't stop this, I'm going to …' They make their love conditional. 'You stop this or else!' There is no definition or consistency in the threat of 'Or else!' Parents are withholding love because the child is not being obedient.

So what happens when the child grows up? You are that grown-up child. We all have this ingrained in us because this is all we heard when we were little, 'No, don't touch! Stop! Get away from that! Mind me or else!' So, now we are adults, and we get a business idea. The first thing that pops into our heads is, 'I can't' because we grew up thinking 'I can't! Mom is going to yell at me. Another 'no' is coming.' And a child who invents a fantastical idea hears, 'Well now, how are you going to do that? I can't afford it, so where are you going to get the money to do that?'[30] Although, as we learned earlier, no one should be expected to know the "how"; we just need to teach our children to decide "what" they want and help them go after it.

The grooves of "I can't" run deeper than the Grand Canyon and spread out just as wide through our lives. We start thinking of all the reasons why we can't. "I don't have the money. It costs too much. It's too far away. It's my genetics. I'm not smart enough. My hair isn't the right color. The sky is blue." You get the idea. We hope you are starting to realize this is a paradigm that was drilled into you as a little child with all those no, no, no's. That was the first word we heard repeatedly. It filters into everything we think and do. As adults with big ideas, we have to fight those constant, debilitating thoughts. This is why we have to sit and think, "Okay, if I have all these reasons why I can't, then by the Law of Polarity, I must be able to think of all the reasons why I *can*. We have to relearn and retrain ourselves as a result.

> **Why is it that we'll spend hundreds or thousands of dollars on physical workout equipment but not a single penny on mental workout equipment?**

Why is it that we'll spend hundreds or thousands of dollars on physical workout equipment but not a single penny on mental workout equipment? As our book title states, what you don't fix, your kids will inherit. What is potentially sabotaging their success is how *you* think. You have the potential within you to stop that which does not facilitate growth and give your child the necessary tools and firm footing to build their own life. You have what they need. Are you ready to bring it forward? Doing so, however, requires effort to overcome the obstacles set before you. These barricades are often in the form of paradigms or limiting beliefs about our situations, our circumstances, and ourselves.

We learn to look at the excuses we have made for ourselves or have taken personally from the comments of well meaning others. Often, these people can be family members or our spouse or significant other. These are people who truly love us and want to prevent us from experiencing disappointment, pain, and failure. And they are the people who, unknowingly, hold us back from our greatest potential and our greatest dreams. We contend that failure does not exist. Each "failure" we think we experience can be turned into a learning experience and redirected. Remember, Thomas Edison failed over 10,000 times when inventing the light bulb, but when he was asked about his failures, he responded, "I have not failed; I've just found 10,000 ways that won't work." Accepting responsibility for your limiting beliefs, which hold you back, is the first step to successful parenting.

Now is the time to let go of some of these negative beliefs about yourself. This helps you become aware of the place from which these beliefs stem. When you let go, you begin to release these negative beliefs and replace them with positive, and life-affirming beliefs. We know how useful this is because we have done it in our own lives. When we decided we wanted to pass our new knowledge on to our children, we realized the parents of the world could benefit from this information as well, so we decided to write our book and build additional programs that give parents the tools they need to raise vibrant, creative, thinking children.

The Checklist

If home inspectors showed up without their checklist, they would not be able to perform their job properly. You can't measure progress if you don't have a plan. We set goals because we believe that this Universe is like a big catalog. We can ask, and we can receive. A lot of people don't believe that. They think life is just happens by chance. We don't think it is like that. We've seen so many parents who said, "I want to do this, I want to do that," but they really don't want it if they are not prepared for the sacrifices. You have to give up something of a lower nature to receive something of a higher nature. For instance, writing this book was one of our goals, and we had to make certain sacrifices (sleep). If we really want our goals, we have to be willing to do anything to attain them. Focus determines direction. As the old saying goes, "Where attention goes, energy flows." In other words, the things you spend your time thinking about will multiply. What do you continually think about at work—the problems, the unfairness, your low paycheck? Or do you think about helping others, finding solutions, and creating opportunities?

> **Thomas Edison failed over 10,000 times when inventing the light bulb, but when he was asked about his failures, he responded, "I have not failed, I've just found 10,000 ways that won't work."**

Instead of competing with everyone else and trying to look to outside reasons for your perceived lack of success, focus on your own ability. Be honest with yourself. With a positive attitude, you become a happier person. When you are happier and focusing on how you can do better, you improve the lives of both you and your children. Don't set them up for difficulties later in life by complaining about a myriad of things. Create within yourself a positive attitude and continue to make yourself better, little by little. As your children see you improving yourself, you set a positive example for them. Show them how to bring out the greatness that lies within them.

We have learned that one of the best methods to teach your children to prepare for the future is to set goals.[5] We haven't figured out why so many people don't set goals even though they know that successful people regularly write their goals down on paper. "Goal setting is an important part of a successful person's life. It is critical that you take the time to establish clear goals. This takes thought and an honest self-assessment. Everybody has to have a goal.

> We got a GPS recently because we were tired of driving in circles and getting lost. It's sort of like that in life. If you have no plan, you are driving in circles. You need a clear vision of where you want to be."[26] We have family goals, like going to Hawaii for our 20th wedding anniversary, traveling across the world promoting our book, and visiting every water park along the way.

When the entire family is involved in the goal-setting process, it focuses more energy toward achieving the intended goal. The best method to reach a goal is to see the end in mind and work your way backwards. This is what you want to see happen: what is it going to take to make that happen? Are you willing to do what it's going to take, and when are you willing to do it? What are those exact steps? If you don't know the exact steps, figure out the steps you can see and then live in the question of, "What do I need to get to the next step?" You'll be amazed by what crosses your path when you're looking for the solution.

Go for the goals that stretch your abilities and require a high level of creativity and energy to conquer. You will never achieve great things without challenges. There is an enormous power in having goals in your daily life. There is an analogy of a ship out at sea without a compass and sailing aimlessly from port to port. Whatever happens does so by the winds of chance. But when you are able to harness the winds of life through goals and a really good sail, you can use them to propel you forward in the direction you want.[5]

We once thought accomplishing goals wasn't for us. We made remarks like, "Oh, that's for other people. Other people can go and do amazing things, but we are meant to live our humble, simple life, just being parents and living day in and day out and waiting for the kids to go to college before our life really starts." Once we started to set goals, we realized how great our life could be right now.

"Goal setting is having something big, something that stretches you out of your comfort zone, and then creating bite-sized chunks that you can do from day to day, and week to week, to make that huge goal a reality. Just like the saying, 'How do you eat a whale? One bite at a time.'"[19]

Goals that don't challenge you move you sideways, not forward. You need to get out of your comfort zone and force yourself to learn new and difficult skills. Stretch yourself and be serious about what you want to achieve. Being serious about a goal means that you are willing to take responsibility to achieve that goal. You are dedicating yourself to self-imposed deadlines for tasks and evaluating your own progress along the way. When you think about setting goals, it is easy to fall into the mindset of just saying that you want to be successful in the next five years. Or in ten years, you want to retire. The next five and ten years are going to happen whether or not you set goals. The odds are pretty high that, without goals, you will be in a very similar place as you are in now.

You have to be looking for the clues from the Universe because they never come with a neon sign.

You have to have a burning desire to achieve your goal. Thinking "It would be nice if ..." isn't going to cut it. You have to plan ahead because the world isn't going to wait for you. The world is changing so fast that you have to have a game plan. As long as you continue to think about your goals, the Universe will deliver clues to your next step. You have to be looking for the clues from the Universe because they never come with a neon sign. They come numerous ways like an email that piques your interest, a billboard message that you pass while diving, a casual comment made by a friend, a dream in the middle of the night, or a thought that pops into your head through your Intuition. The responsibility you take toward the accomplishment of your goals plays an important role in whether or not you reach them. If you don't decide to follow through no matter what and then stick to that decision, you will never reach what you desire.

In order to achieve success and the life of your dreams, you have to see yourself accomplishing your goals and living how you would live once your goals have been reached. Your goals should create a burning desire deep within you. If you don't truly desire something, then it is easy to become distracted and fail to follow through. It makes sense that your first step in goal setting is to have a goal that you really want and to create the feelings you will have once the goal has been achieved. The stronger the feelings, the more quickly your goals manifest.[5]

One of the techniques we learned from Bob Proctor is how to find your Goal. If money were not an option, would you buy it? Would you do it? If the answer is yes, then that is your goal.

On the next page, make a list of all the things you want to have, do, or be. It does not matter how ridiculous or impossible the ideas seem. If they pop into your head, write them down. Do not disregard any idea because you currently do not have the money to make it reality.

MY GOAL LIST:

_____
_____
_____
_____
_____
_____
_____
_____
_____
_____
_____
_____
_____
_____
_____
_____

When your list is complete, read it to a friend or loved one, and tell them about each item. When you are finished, ask them to tell you which ones you really seemed excited about. Keep working on it until you have narrowed it down to your one main goal. When we did this exercise, we learned that we both had basically the same goal of creating magical learning experiences by world schooling our children and exploring the world in first-class style.

It is critical that you spend time visualizing yourself achieving your goal. We carry around our goals on a goal card and read them several times a day, creating constant pictures in our minds. If you can't picture your goals, then you probably won't achieve them. Focus on your goals and ask yourself these questions:

- What can I do each day to achieve my goals?
- Am I willing to take responsibility to accomplish these tasks?

Here are our current goal cards:

Cory: By December 30, 2011, I am so happy and grateful now that our best selling books, tools, and other resources are providing a beneficial service to hundreds of thousands of people, helping them raise happy and healthy children who know that they can be, have, and do anything they desire. By helping others we generate income that provides us with everything we want. We are traveling the world giving people useful tools and information while creating magical learning experiences with our family.

Anamarie: By December 30, 2011, I'm so happy and grateful now that our best-selling book and multiple sources of income bring us in excess of $10,000 per month, Cory is working at home with me, and we're helping thousands of people raise successful children. We're traveling the globe first class, world-schooling our children, promoting our books, and creating memories that result in, "Mom, that was the best day ever!"

Now that you've reviewed what we have on our goal cards, take a moment and create your own in the space below. Start by setting an accomplishment date. Take the time you think you're going to need and cut it in half. If you set the date to a reasonable time like two years, it's not going to push you, but if you change that date to one year, now it might seem impossible, which motivates you. Activities will fill the time allotted; you really want to turn on the heat by setting a crazy goal with an even crazier date of accomplishment.

BY_____, 20___ I AM SO HAPPY AND GRATEFUL NOW THAT ...

_____

_____

_____

_____

_____

_____

_____

_____

_____

Carry your goal card in your pocket or purse all the time.[5] We have a friend who sleeps with her goal card under her pillow. Pull out your goal card and read it several times a day. Think about how you are going to feel when all of this manifests in your life. Create action steps for accomplishing each goal. Identify what you need and how long it will take. Some of what you identify may seem impossible. That's okay because it's what makes this process so darn fun. As you identify goals, it's a really good idea to define the most important steps that must happen for your goals to become a reality. You can't build a house without a blueprint, and goals are no different. If you don't have a blueprint for building and completing your goals, you will have a difficult time manifesting them. However, don't worry if you don't have all the answers right now. With each step toward your goal, you raise your Level of Awareness and move forward.

"When we set a goal, it is very helpful to break it down into three items that we want to do to accomplish that goal. Make the first item something you know you can *absolutely* accomplish. Next, write down something you can *probably* do. Last is the biggest part of getting the goal accomplished: write down something that you are *not sure* you will do. Here are the steps applied to when we wrote this book:

1. Get an idea and create an outline,
2. Write five topics under each chapter
3. Write three chapters a week.

Another example could be when cleaning a room:

1. Pick the papers and toys up from the floor,
2. Organize one drawer, and
3. Clean out the closet.

In your mind, starting the first task spurs you on to do the second. By then, you are on a roll and you have a strong desire to get it done."[24]

The next step is to take action. Your goal will only come if you are actually working toward that goal. You can visualize to your heart's content, but if you aren't actually getting up and taking steps toward your goal, the goal will not move toward you. "It is important to do what you know, not what you feel. Orient your goals based on where you know you want to go, not what you feel today. This moves you in the direction that you want to go because you will never feel like it 24/7. Doing what you know leads you in the direction you want to go. Don't base your decisions upon what you feel."[22]

> **We can't set a goal bigger than our paradigm until we believe in ourselves.**

Remember from the Stickman image in Chapter Two? The subconscious mind produces feelings, which are manifested as vibrations in your body, which originated from your thoughts in your conscious mind. So if you're in a negative vibration, your feelings always work against you. "Doing what you know comes out of your vision and the appointment you keep with yourself and the sense of destiny you have. This becomes critical when guiding your children's thinking to make decisions based upon what they must do, not based upon what they feel. They haven't yet learned how to control their emotions.

> We've started training our kids how to move toward their goals, 'What is it you know you need to do right now?' ... 'Well, I don't feel like it.' ... 'I understand you don't feel like it. Now that we got that out of the way, I agree with you 100 percent, but what is it you know you must do?' ... 'I need to practice.' 'Okay, so let's get going.'"[22]

In order to accomplish our goals on a daily basis, every evening we also create a list of six actions to do the next day. This has been phenomenal in our life. Remember, setting goals involves risk. That means risking a wrong move, a bad decision, a loss of some money, or even a major setback. It also means that you must be adaptable to changing circumstances. You are only defeated if you label yourself as such, and you stop pursuing your goals. Many of the most successful people in this world have previously lost everything, sometimes many times. They did not give up. They looked at their "failure" as only a temporary setback, and they looked for what they could learn from the experience. Jack Canfield tells of a man who lost over $100 million on a deal and, looking back at the experience, only laughs, saying that he turned the information that he learned from that loss into an $800 million deal the next time around. "Failures" in our lives are just God's way of helping us learn and grow. We only fail if we give up, so learn from your setbacks and keep pursuing your goals. When you have a full belief in yourself, you will accomplish your goals. Renew your belief in yourself and your goal. Giving up is not the right message to send to your children. They have to see you play it out fully, 100 percent.

You still have to juggle things like your job, family, bills, and saving for the future. Out of necessity, there will be times when certain goals take a temporary backseat to others. At these times, your responsibility is tested. Keep focused, and remember that no matter how difficult times may seem, with a determined mindset and an attitude of responsibility, you will achieve your goals.

We can't set a goal bigger than our paradigm until we believe in ourselves. Sometimes you achieve your goal and sometimes you don't, but know that when you have a vision and work toward it, how you handle not making it is just as important as the journey toward the goal. The frustration when the goal hasn't manifested is really nothing more than wavering belief in yourself. Your past doesn't define you. Mistakes, relationships, and your previous actions are merely a collection of experiences in your memory. You are not your job, car, home, or financial portfolio. These are just possessions that can come and go. Once you understand that your past and your possessions are only external labels that hold no security, you can move forward with a realistic, confident belief in yourself. Your security is within you. No matter who rejects you, no matter how many times you "fail," you are still you. Those rejections and failures are just experiences. You learn from experience.[30]

Everything Is Working

Deepak Chopra says, "Success in life could be defined as the continued expansion of happiness and the progressive realization of worthy goals. Success is the ability to fulfill your desires with effortless ease. And yet success, including the creation of wealth, has always been considered to be a process that requires hard work, and it is often considered to be at the expense of others. We need a more spiritual approach to success and to affluence, which is the abundant flow of all good things to you." Although earning adequate money to be secure and comfortable is certainly on the short list of goals, other achievements usually have a higher priority. Is success having a happy family life, children who make us proud, good health, or love? Success is all of the above, and none of the above. The definition of success is often difficult to explain. Sounds strange, we know, but your success depends on what you want in life not what society deems acceptable. Success is different for every person. Each of us places different values on different areas of our life.

Like everyone else, you want to be successful in all areas of your life. What is your definition of success? Write your answer in the space provided.

MY DEFINITION OF SUCCESS

Health

Business

Family

Financial

Daily Life

Spiritual

Personal

Relationships

For more writing space please visit
www.ParentOutLoud.com/STEP to download your free Play-Book.

Now that you have a better definition of what success means to you, take this opportunity to assess your individual goals, broaden your definition of success, and identify the characteristics that will help you succeed. Finding your own personal success involves finding what makes you happy and then mastering it. Set your goals and see them through to the end. The moment you set your goal and begin pursuing it, you are successful. Earl Nightingale, known as the Dean of Personal Development, says, "Success is the pursuit of a worthy goal." Success is about being who you are and pursuing what you want in life. Don't let anyone except yourself have power over you by telling you how to live. There are many kinds of desire, but one that is held by most people is the desire for success. Unfortunately, many people strive for success even at the expense of themselves. What good is success if you gain the whole world and lose yourself?

> **Earl Nightingale says, "Success is the pursuit of a worthy goal."**

Every day, we need to ask ourselves the question: "Am I getting any closer to my true definition of success in life? Am I making this world a better place to live?" If the answer is no, then you may need to reassess whether your actions and goals are in alignment and in harmony with your true beliefs. Life rewards us in direct proportion to our contribution. The earlier we find our meaning of success, the better life is. This is true not only as an individual but also for our family, business, and world.[5]

Once we've found our definition of success, we also become aware of when we need to take a stand. That is the time we start making the right decisions for long-term gain rather than making the wrong decisions for short-term gain. Wisdom and maturity lead to greater understanding of major issues. Every success leads to a better world for not only you but others as well. For us, success means the realization of everyone's hopes and dreams, not just our own. True success happens on the inside. We encourage you to develop your own sense of what success means and stop comparing yourself to others; before you know it, your self-esteem skyrockets, and your life will be your own.

Match Your Blueprint

It is important for you to take control of your thoughts and sense of self because your outlook can either change your life for the better or leave you captive to your conditions. This is true especially when thoughts are expressed in both the spoken and written word. Throughout history, philosophers, theologians, scientists and other wise men and women have disagreed on many things, but one thing they do agree on is that "We become what we think about." What are your thoughts? How many times have you called yourself stupid, idiot, lazy, insensitive, careless, and so on? What do you think about the most? Are your thoughts filled with possibilities, energy, and prosperity, or are they filled with hardship, competition, lack, and limitations?

We become what we think about.

> When we find ourselves flipping over into more of a victim role, we stop and say, "You know what? That's not right. We made that choice. You did not cause us to get angry. I chose to let your behavior bother me." We talk to our children about this as well, that their siblings, friends, peers, teachers and other people, even parents, may say something that is very upsetting. You can choose to reject anything that is going to make you feel bad about yourself.
>
> Lately, we have been telling 12-year-old Justine that when her brothers say something to annoy her that she is "giving all of her power away." She chooses to let their comments annoy

her. What we create in our lives we create from our thinking. Everything that exists in this world came about because someone thought about it. The good thing is that we have the ability to choose what we think. We can consciously accept or reject any thought that comes into our mind. Since so much that happens in a child's life is so dramatic, we have found it extremely helpful to ask our children, "Does it really matter?" "Yes!" "No, seriously. Does it really matter?" "Well, no."

Shift your focus from thinking that you must get something (money, people, a job, a thing, a healthier body, etc) to being grateful for what you do have at this moment. Our focus must be on how we can develop our unique talents so that we learn to use them in the most effective way we can wherever we are right now. Focus on giving your all in the work that you do, your family life, and your relationships right now, and watch how your life changes course toward what you desire. If you had been feeling you were a victim of your thoughts and circumstances, a focus shift is a very important realization. By following our guidelines, you will see your new and better life unfold.

No Cracked Windows

Earlier, we mentioned that if you can't picture your goals, then you probably won't achieve them. Along with our goal cards, we create vision boards. A vision board is nothing more than a poster board, corkboard, or even a notebook covered or filled with pictures and

Believing is Seeing.

images of your desires. These are very powerful because once an image is embedded into your subconscious, then it becomes reality. Ours is in our home office. We've all heard the phrase seeing is believing. In our case, we disagree. To us, Believing is Seeing.

You miss a powerful ingredient when you do not include the visual. You may see something in your mind, but how often do you focus on that? Using a vision board, goal board, or a dream board keeps your vision right in front of you in a room. Whenever you wake up or you go to bed, by the nature of where it is positioned, you are always keeping a visual reminder of what you want. So when you are visualizing, and you are practicing visualization, it is there to excite you. On those days where what you want seems to be further away, or you have taken a step backwards, or your plans haven't come out the way you wanted them to, it is there to encourage you.

Visualization is the art of being able to see with our mind. Some refer to this as their imagination. When you visualize or use your imagination, you create mental images, which are sustained and energized by intense concentration. The concept is simple: what your mind sees and is made to believe becomes your reality. Scientific research has proven that your subconscious can't tell if something is real or imagined, and your subconscious is where your beliefs are held. Mental visualization creates a state, situation, or environment that you want to physically manifest in your life. Your imagination is a very powerful tool to help you achieve what you want in life, and a vision board is a tool for your conscious mind to use to give you images to visualize and record into your subconscious. The more you visualize these images, the more clear the images become in your mind. You probably have used visualization many times during your life in one way or another without even realizing it. Think about the last time you shopped for a new apartment or home. While standing in the empty room, did you visualize where your sofas, dining table and entertainment center would go in the spaces?

Here's another example. Think about the enormous amount of time you've probably wasted in your life complaining. How often have you replayed certain events where you thought you were mistreated or undervalued over and over in your mind? Or how many times have you remembered the winning home run you hit in high school, your wedding day, or the birth of your children. Every time you think about these times, you are using visualization.

The concept behind visualization is using your power of thought because thoughts are vibrations, and your thoughts actually affect people and your environment.[5] You have probably walked into a room and, without a word being exchanged, you could tell that a particular person was in a really bad mood, or that someone had recently had a traumatic event happen. You can actually pick up the other person's vibration. Use this to your advantage as well when faced with any type of negativity or unpleasant environment. If you sense an argument coming with your spouse or family member, visualize a tactful and reasonable solution in your mind, which sets up a more positive vibration and affects both of your actions. Visualization allows you to formulate a positive response in your head, which flows out of your mouth, ending in a pleasant conversation. People are generally responsive to thoughts, behaviors, and feelings; they typically react appropriately and accordingly. You can't just sit on your couch and wish for a happier life. You have to actually believe that you attract to you everything you need for that happier life and that you will have the life you are seeing for yourself.

For visualization to be effective you must use all of your senses and put as much emotion into it as you can.

Understanding how the mind works really helps children practice their visualization. It's helpful to draw out the Stickman for them so they can see how the mind and body works together. Then once they have seen it and understand, you can ask, "What are you working on now? How are you using your Will to speed up the things you want?"

For example, let's say one of our boys wanted to make the starting lineup on the basketball team. We would ask, "'What are you doing at night when you go to sleep? Are you visualizing that you're in the starting lineup?'" Once they understand the basics of how visualization works, you can do activities to help guide them."[2]

Working the Home Theater System

Understanding the power of visualization is important. Otherwise, why would you or your children choose to visualize? They need to understand that they are visualizing so they are increasing that rate of vibration in their body. This draws something to them much more quickly. While the average person may really want something but have no clue how to bring it to themselves, we want our children to create by design so that when they are going to bed at night, they are visualizing for a reason.

One of the most important things to realize is that for visualization to be effective, you must use all of your senses and put as much emotion into it as you can.[5] When you practice visualization, you need to imagine not only how something looks but also how it feels, sounds, smells, and tastes. You must imagine what emotions you experience when you have that thing or event, whatever it may be. The more sensory input you have, the richer and stronger your visualization is and the stronger the vibration you set up. The stronger the vibration, the stronger the attraction and the quicker the people, circumstances, and/or connections you need to manifest your desire come to you. Here are a few suggestions to help make your visualization more powerful and successful:

- Begin your visualization in a relaxed state.

- See, hear, and feel as much detail as possible. (A guided visualization CD may be helpful when beginning this process.)

- Maintain control over your imagery.

- To strengthen the effect of your image, make it brighter, more colorful, closer, larger, louder, and sharper.

- Feel the emotions associated with the image, and make them as strong as possible.

- Have fun and enjoy the process.

Visualization is a wonderful mental faculty, and it is one of the most powerful things you can do on a regular basis to help achieve your goals and become the person you want to be. Use this power consciously and continuously to create the kind of future you want for yourself.[5]

Interestingly, most people think that the power of visualization is way too good to be true. Nevertheless, it has been proven that it can and does alter circumstances that affect important events in your life. It is used to attract love, work, and material possessions. Additionally, psychologists use visualization to assist their patients in breaking destructive habits to consequently improve their state of health and sense of well-being.

In addition to changing our thought process, eliminating the negativity, and visualizing for a better life, we also need to be grateful for all that we have. It's easy to drift into focusing on the negative, on problems, and on what isn't working. But what you focus on expands. So focusing on the negative and on problems gets you more negativity and more problems, not the enjoyment and fulfillment you long for. Gratitude includes thankfulness for what we may initially perceive as bad (remember, we need to find the seed of equivalent benefit) as well as the good in our lives.

All Systems Check

In *The Science of Getting Rich*, Wallace D. Wattles writes of the importance of gratitude it is a natural outflow of life. Gratitude opens you up to more things you can be thankful for. Don't curse things that happen. Instead, start blessing the things in your life. This may feel very awkward and fake at first, but gradually, over time, your gratitude becomes strong and deep.

> We have been asked many times how to be grateful, and we cite examples taught at our church to the little babies in Sunday school. "Thank you for my ears so I can hear. Thank you for my eyes so I can see. Thank you for the trees, and thank you for the birds and their beautiful songs." We often find what is taught to small children is also easily embraced by adults. No one wants to be around someone who is always complaining.

Wattles also says that by being grateful, we are drawn closer to God. And since God is the creator of all, by being closer to the power that creates all, we bring those creative energies closer to us, which in turn brings our desires to us more quickly. We are grateful to you, and we are grateful for everything. Gratitude is what makes the Universe flow. We are so grateful for the idea to make this information available to people everywhere. We know that lives will be changed for the better, and we feel so blessed and grateful for this opportunity.

Everything begins with gratitude. Our kids have learned that they get better results when they stay in gratitude. When your children are grateful, they get more privileges. They are improving daily at picking up on our vibration. They know when we're mad even when we want to try and hide it. Author Leslie Householder shares this illustration:

It's funny because we will be on a family outing together and if something has us off—maybe the kids have done something that annoyed us—they can tell that we are on edge and might be getting angry. They know instantly that is going to affect the result they have; it is going to affect whether or not they get the ice cream on the way home. The first thing that happens is the car gets quiet because they don't like us to be angry. We don't like to be angry. The car goes quiet and someone will inevitably remember, "Thank you, Mom and Dad, for taking us." We respond to the gratitude, "You are welcome." All of a sudden, we have softened. They are seeing how, in our family, gratitude changes the vibration. If you can begin to see how gratitude changes your vibration, just imagine what kind of blessings God can send.

A journal of gratitude helps to increase your awareness of how blessed you are in life.

Gratitude is an attitude that we must consciously choose because it makes life better for us and for other people.[5] To incorporate gratitude into your life, we recommend our method. We practice an expression of gratitude by keeping a gratitude journal. At dinnertime or before we go to bed, our family writes one or two items for which we are grateful. By this, we mean we don't just write the same thing each time. We make it a point to note something specific to our current circumstance. A journal of gratitude helps to increase your awareness of how blessed you are in life. Plus, it is a great tool for when someone, or the whole family, is in a negative vibration. During those times, pull out the gratitude journal and read what you have written. The positive vibrations and love you put into the words you have written are reflected back to you and can put you back into a positive state.

Living with gratitude has truly changed our lives. At times, it has not been easy for us to be thankful, but we remain filled with so much energy and inspiration, it is a privilege to be able to have the wisdom and strength to be thankful for the challenges in our lives. Remember: our lives are best, not compared to others, but to our own goals, passions, and desires. We challenge you to make the most of your life with your children. We want you to transform their potential into performance.

Remember: the only way to master any area of your life is through trial and error. Don't be so hard on yourself if things did not turn out the way you wanted them to at first. A positive attitude shifts your vibration and gives you energy as you move forward. When our children flourish, we are at our most vibrant and radiant. This radiant glow is what sets the proud parent apart from the rest. You stand out, and your energy and inspiration is contagious to those around you. Just think, the example you set today may save the life of someone else's child tomorrow!

Are you ready to take action and get moving with designing the life you desire as well as giving your child a strong foundation for success on their own? There are specific actions you can do to put these ideas on paper and literally begin to paint the picture of how you want your life to be. In turn, your children will want to paint the picture of their life. It can be viewed as the creation of a goal card, a vision board, a vision journal, a screen saver, or a running movie for those of you who are computer savvy. It can also be just a simple creative visualization experience where dreaming and meditation help you to focus on what you want and where you hope to go.

As you develop your own picture of "what looks good," remember that goals are personal. You may refer to other's ideas about what looks good, but your good life will not be exactly the same as your brother's or sister's, even though you probably grew up in the same household with the same parents, teachers, and religious instructors. This is something that is uniquely yours. Enjoy the process, too. Remember the fun you had the first time you were allowed to choose the décor for your bedroom? Or you were able to choose the automobile you wanted? This type of plan for your life should be just as much fun. To quote author Peggy McColl; "I was writing my purchase order to the Universe this morning!"

ACTION STEPS

Author Annie Fox shares this powerful exercise.

1. Take out a piece of paper and list your top 10 parenting objectives between now and the time your child turns 18. Most people will say something like "I want them to be self confident, independent in their thinking, to make good financial choices. I want them to be good partners, good friends, trustworthy, honest, good citizens..." List them all.

2. Now list what you are doing every single day to make sure that when it's time for the exit exam at age 18 and they are graduating from your parent university, that they are going to pass your 'Complete Independence' exit exam with flying colors? Whatever you are doing, list it.

Are you actively engaging in opportunities to help your children learn each of the listed qualities in question #1? What might you be doing occasionally that actually undermines your parenting objectives?" For example, you say you want your child to be independent. Are you still making his lunch for him? Are you still waking him up, laying out his clothes the night before and escorting him to the door so that he can catch his ride to school? I'm sorry, but keep that up and you are not in fact fostering independence at all, but just the opposite. You have to think about what you as a parent are really about. You've got a curriculum. You are a teacher! I don't think most parents think about this.

3. List the things you are going to change in order to prepare you children for their exit exam. You know that 18 years is going to pass too quickly.

**For more writing space please visit
www.ParentOutLoud.com/STEP to download your free PlayBook.**

CHAPTER 10

LANDSCAPING

Money is usually attracted, not pursued.

–Jim Rohn

Little Ian wanted something special.

"Well, what are you willing to do to make that happen?" his adoring grandmother asked.

"I am going to sell something," the ten-year-old said.

Natalie smiled. "What are you going to sell?"

"Well, I'm not selling my toys." He looked up into the tree towering above him. "I am selling those coconuts right there." Natalie looked up, seeing that the tree was full of coconuts.

"Ian, those coconuts are *in* the tree," she laughed.

He said, "Mimi, you always told me; you will find a way if you are committed. I *am* committed to getting those coconuts out of that tree."

He convinced his papa to help him get the coconuts out of the tree. They shucked them together, and he filled up his little wagon. He decided to do a little market research by going to the grocery store and found out that they sold coconuts for about $2.

He came back to his grandmother. "Mimi, I am selling them for $3."

"Ian, if they are $2 in the store, what is making you sell them for $3?"

He said, "Well, Mimi, I am *delivering* them."

"Okay, go for it and see what happens," she said, beaming with pride.

He practiced what he was going to say and then headed out to the beckoning neighborhood.

A few hours later, he returned, radiating with joy, "I did it Mimi! I sold every coconut in my wagon!"

Natalie was so proud of her grandson while they shopped together. She knew that he would deeply value what he bought with his money because he earned it. This is one of the most important things we can do with kids.[26]

Planting

If you've ever built a house, you know that the final aspect of the building process is the landscaping. A lush green lawn is the icing on the cake, so to speak. Most people don't realize just how much "green" it actually takes to get that beautifully landscaped yard. Landscaping also has an important purpose. It prevents Mother

Nature from eroding your land onto your neighbor's property. So in our final chapter, we'd like to discuss the importance of keeping your house green … with cash, that is. Financial responsibility isn't just for parents; we need to teach our children how to manage money as well. You can't spoil kids. The most important thing to teach them is that they are no better than anybody, and they are no worse than anybody. They have to have a good image of themselves.

> We teach them that all the money in the Universe is available to them; all they have to do is earn it. If they really want to earn money, they should have multiple sources of income. We're of the opinion that there is lots of money out there, and you should have what you need to do what you want to do. We're fostering a healthy respect for money, and our kids know they have to earn it.

People have an idea of what the perfect amount of money is for them. For some, this may be a million dollars in the bank. Others may want enough to live comfortably and stay out of debt. Think about what your perfect amount of money is. The most obvious step to financial independence is to earn more money. One of the first thoughts that may come into your mind is to either work longer hours at your current job or maybe get a second job. On the surface, these may seem like the most effective ways to increase your cash flow leading to financial independence, but they are not. We don't believe that trading your time for money is the most effective way to earn it; neither should you or your children. There is only so much time you can trade for money, but we will teach you a different, better way. But first, you must understand that before you can become financially independent, you need to change your mindset about money.

You need to re-evaluate the way you look at earning money. In Chapter Nine, we talked about developing a positive attitude, and the same is true with money. Before you can teach your children about money, you first have to develop a healthy relationship and attitude toward money yourself. Contrary to what you've heard, the love of money is not greed. Money is a magnifier. More money makes you *more* of what *you* already are. So, start giving while you have a little. It's all about giving because success is a paradox. The more you give, the more you receive. It is not possible to *make* money. The only people who make money work at the U.S. Mint. Everybody else must *earn* money. You earn money by providing value first. Chess mentor Orrin Hudson says, "Add the value first. Give, Add Value, Serve, Help, Go above and beyond, Arrive early, Stay late, Give, Give, Give ... Delay ... delay ... delay ... Then you get money back. Money is a byproduct. Money only comes after you add value."

The most important thing to teach them is that they are no better than anybody and they are no worse than anybody.

The Value of Green

"It's important to understand that money is not real. The value is based on the production of the person. The one true principle is that value follows value, or, in other words, what you give is what you receive. This exchange principle is ever present and therefore, a dollar is only a representation of value. As a result, you can exchange all kinds of things that aren't necessarily dollars. There is a deeper principle to learn aside from just the money. Early on, chores are one of the best ways to help children learn this. But you have to create a little bit of autonomy with your children first. Children must learn that wealth can't be attributed to luck. If you attribute luck to it, you are going to lose it, which is why people who win the lottery never keep it, right? They haven't learned how to be a steward of their money."[7]

Hired Help?

At some point, children and parents must learn how to exchange value and work. When you give an allowance, it shouldn't just be like a salary. "If you start giving them a salary-type of allowance, you are going to notice that they ask exactly what many adults would ask: 'How can I do the least amount of work for the most money? How can I just do the minimum? How can I just barely get by with it?' Just giving your children money enables them and creates an entitlement mentality."[7]

> In our family, allowance is tied to certain chores. We have some chores that are just expected because they are part of the family unit; we all pitch in. But just like in the adult world, we teach our children that the money we earn is in exchange for a valuable service that we provided to someone else.

"A great aspect about being an entrepreneur is you really learn that the world gives you feedback very quickly compared to a normal job because if you are not offering value, people won't exchange dollars with you. If you do that at a normal job, they will eventually fire you. Children have to understand very quickly, which is why it's a great idea to get a job. This could be something as simple as getting a lemonade stand or whatever they desire to do, but helping them understand that the only way to receive more value and increase stewardship is to be a good steward over those resources. When it comes to money, you have to understand that the source of money is not money. The source is the value of products or services that you have created for society."[7]

Truthful Labels

Imagine you've spent two years creating a striking blue and white flowering border along the edge of your driveway. While shopping at the nursery, you find a package of ten rare Blue Amiable

Triumph Tulip bulbs. You've been looking for several months and rush home to plant them. The next six months seem to crawl by as you wait for spring. Finally, the bulbs have started to grow, and you know that tomorrow they will bloom. The glory of a perfect day is shattered when you discover that your rare blue tulips are lipstick red! Imagine the frustration; how could this happen? Somehow those bulbs were mislabeled. We create this same silent frustration in our children when we aren't 100 percent truthful and mislabel things for our children. You may be thinking, "But I always tell the truth!" Do you? Read on; you might be surprised.

Anytime you walk by a toy store or department store, depending upon the ages of your kids, you inevitably hear "I want ... Buy me this ...!" And for some of you, the words "Money doesn't grow on trees," "Do you think I'm made of money?" or "We can't afford that" may have come out of your mouth. But take a moment next time and think about what these words are really saying. In all reality, you're telling your child that there isn't enough money now, and there won't be enough in the future either. Is this true?

> We've been to the toy section of several stores many times and heard our children say, "I want this, I want that. Can you buy it for us?"
>
> One year ago our response was, "We can't afford it."
>
> This resulted in more whining and begging. Why? Because they just watched us spend $100 at the grocery store, so our words were not consistent with our behavior. After doing some personal growth study and increasing our awareness, we realized that our children weren't asking for yachts and airplanes.
>
> We decided to replace "We can't afford it" with "Yes, we could purchase that, but today we're not choosing to spend our money that way. We're choosing to spend the $100 that you want for that toy on the groceries for this week so you can eat dinner. If you would like to spend your money on that, you can."

"But I don't have that much money," one child would reply.

"That's okay. Let's figure out how you can earn that extra money."

What type of effect do you think that type of response is going to have on them later in life? Now, our children aren't living with a constant feeling that we don't have enough money. They now experience that we are stewards of our money and are making wise choices. Now, they live with the idea that if they want it, they just need to *decide* if they really want it and then use their imagination to create ideas to earn the money. So the next time you find yourself in this situation, pause and take a moment before responding. This situation presents a great opportunity to teach an important lesson on how to develop a wealth consciousness. Most of us live our entire lives with a consciousness of lack, or worse, we're taught that money is the root of all evil. If you go back and reread the Bible verse you'll see that it is misquoted. The verse actually states that the *love of* money is the root of all evil.

You must acquire the habits and skills of managing a small amount of money before you can have a large amount.

Wanting wealth is not wrong or bad. It does not make you shallow, superficial, or evil. Your wanting wealth doesn't mean that all you care about is money. That's not the case. The desire for wealth is actually the desire for a fuller, more abundant life.

Controlling Growth

In the Pacific Northwest, wild blackberries grow everywhere, so much so that they are considered a weed. Birds love eating the berries, so they are constantly spreading the seeds. If blackberry sprouts are left unchecked, they will take over your entire yard. The same is true with neglecting to take control of your finances; you're creating some thorny issues.

Author T. Harv Eker writes in *Secrets of the Millionaire Mind*, "The single biggest difference between financial success and financial failure is how well you manage your money. It's simple: to master money, you must *manage* money ... Poor people either mismanage their money, or they avoid the subject of money altogether ... It comes down to this: either you control money, or it controls you. To control money, you must manage it ... You must acquire the habits and skills of managing a small amount of money before you can have a large amount ... Money is a big part of your life, and when you learn how to get your finances under control, all areas of your life will soar." We can relate to these quotes.

> **Teach your children that the universe is unlimited and that if they truly believe, it is possible to have any amount of money they desire.**

We have gone in cycles of ignoring our money and not reconciling accounts for up to a year, to meeting weekly to make sure that we reconciled everything and that every dollar was accounted for. Our paradigms showed up during those weekly meetings, and we became extremely upset when we overspent for the month and had to dip into savings. This foul mood could last up to 72 hours and affected the entire family. It took time to break through the paradigm that "it is easier to ignore our money," and we're so grateful that we did.

So many parents train their children to believe there is only so much wealth to go around, and the majority of it has already been accounted for. This is not true. Teach your children that the Universe is unlimited and that if they truly believe, it is possible to have any amount of money they desire. They can have what they want. To do this, however, you have to begin teaching your children about the basics of money when they first begin to develop an awareness about it. In a child's world, money comes from Mom and Dad's pockets, but they need to realize that they, too, are capable of earning their own money. After they gain confidence with this knowledge, they begin to understand that money is readily available whenever it is needed.

When we speak of wealth, we don't mean having just enough to pay your off your mortgage, credit cards, and cars. Thinking this way is what we like to call the "just enough mindset." This thought process prevents you from acquiring a vast amount of wealth because you are content with having just enough. Why would you be satisfied with just a little wealth, when you have been granted the use of the entire Universe for your benefit? Every man, woman, and child deserves to have money. All you have to do is ask. *Ask and you shall receive.* The Universe responds to those who ask. If we knew of the wealth that we're not receiving because we're not asking, we would most definitely change our behavior.

So why don't we ask? Mainly because we're afraid the person we're asking will say no. How do you know until you ask? Look at it this way: you already aren't getting what you want, so what would it hurt to ask?

> We discovered this while creating this book. We had to ask our friends if they knew people who fit certain parameters in order to interview them for the book. If we didn't ask, no one would have volunteered anything.

Another reason for people not asking for what they want is they are afraid that they are unworthy. No one is unworthy of having money. No one person is better than another. We all are equal in terms of deserving wealth. We are all worthy. This is a hard concept for some people to accept.

Interestingly enough, we've spent the majority of this book discussing techniques to teach your children how to live a better life. In this case, however, we can learn from our children. They live by the principle that it never hurts to ask ... and ask, and ask.

How many times have your children asked for a cookie or dessert, over and over and over, until you finally give it to them? Rather than giving in, teach your children how to ask regularly.

> When we learned this concept, we started to notice how many "asking" opportunities were passing us. "I'm thirsty," and one of us would proceed to get a glass of water. "I'm hot," and we would take off their sweater. As attentive parents, we need to cater to our children less and teach them to ask for what they need. We now respond with, "Use your words and ask for what you want." After a while, our kids started to say, "May I have a glass of water," instead of telling us they were thirsty.

Saving Seeds

Benjamin Franklin once said, "An investment in knowledge always pays the best interest." Answering your children's questions honestly and in terms they'll understand can help them begin life on a sound financial footing. We believe in tithing and saving. We also believe in putting money aside for others. How many adults don't save or tithe? Imagine children learning about that from a young age. They learn early on that you always live on less than what you earn. It's the only way that you are ever going to truly prosper financially. All of our children are savers. They research what they want, and they understand about saving for it.

We can learn from our children. They live by the principle that it never hurts to ask... and ask, and ask.

With our younger children, we learned a great exercise from parenting coach Leigh Scott, which teaches three-to-six-year-old children how to budget money by giving them a pile of cookies on Tuesday and Thursday. If they ate all of their cookies Tuesday, they wouldn't get anymore until Thursday. They came screaming to us in the middle of the week. "I'm all out of cookies. I want more cookies." We told them that we'd be happy to give them more on Thursday. The next week, the same scenario: they gobbled up their cookies the same day they received them. They cried and begged for more, but we held steadfast to our rule. By the third week, they totally understood the concept of budgeting. So, even before we started giving them money, they understood the concept.

"Then, as they are older, they are getting their allowance; they're starting to make choices about their clothes. Several of our interviews taught us that the quicker you can let go and turn decisions over to your children, the better you are preparing them for your 'Complete Independence' exit exam. Whatever budget you have planned for your children's clothes or for their books and so on, turn it all over to them as soon as possible. This is because you want them to make spending mistakes when they are young. When they're older, spending mistakes have a much bigger consequence in the form of credit card debt."[4]

When we looked at creating an allowance for our kids, we wanted them to get an allowance based on certain activities that they did. This helped them feel powerful because now they would have their own money that they earned by exchanging their time. They would be making their own decisions. The first step was for them to create a habit by making sure they understood that a portion of every dollar they earned is theirs to keep today and into the future. And we mean every dollar, including gift monies received. The savings aspect helps them manage the flow of their finances. We wanted them to understand that in order to take advantage of opportunities, you want make sure that you have access to money you've saved.

We modified money author T. Harv Eker's six Money Jars concept. Ten percent is for education. This is for college and personal growth courses. Ten percent is for gifts for others, birthdays, and Christmas. Ten percent goes into giving. The children choose where they want to donate this money, whether it's church or charitable organizations. Ten percent goes to spending. This is money they must spend every week and gives them the sense that they constantly have money flowing into their lives. Fifty percent goes into long-term savings for spending (LTSS). This is for the next big toy or game that our children are working to earn.

The last ten percent goes into their financial freedom account (FFA). This is like their golden goose. The money is invested and never touched. This money continues to earn interest forever, like the golden goose continues to lay golden eggs for the length of her life. The interest is constantly rolled over until a predetermined time. Then, only the interest is spent from this account and is considered one source of income.

> According to Paul Demazo in his article "Wealth Creation: The Miracles of Compounding Interest" on FreeMoneyFinance. com, "Compound interest is the greatest mathematical discovery of all time,' said Dr. Albert Einstein. The results are determined by time, not just how much you invest! Time really is magic. The Rule of 72 developed by Dr. Albert Einstein is an easy way to estimate how long it will take for your money to double with annual compounding. (Divide 72 by the percentage growth rate.) For example, with a 15 percent return your money doubles every 4.8 years. Round it to five years (for simplicity's sake). This means a $5,000 one-time investment made at birth by parents and grandparents would grow to $2,560,000 when the child is 45 years old! This awesome result is based on two major factors—compounding interest and time.

Wealth is a matter of choice, and you alone must make the choice. At the same time, you can be showing your children all sorts of different ways to earn money. Getting a job out of college isn't their only option. Encourage them to start their own businesses and to make investments in their younger years that provide financial security.

Creating a Butterfly Garden

Butterflies add so much delicate beauty to your property, but you must attract them by choosing the right plants. They freely come in, do what they choose, and then flit right out of your yard. The entrepreneurial spirit is very similar in our children. It must be attracted and nurtured.

"Everyone can benefit from the tax advantages of a home-based business. An increasing number of us today are seeing the need for a Plan B because we can't count on our jobs being there tomorrow. Job security just doesn't exist anymore. Having a home-based business can increase peace of mind with another stream of income and provide additional, little known, amazing tax benefits.

Plus, there is so much that children learn about, like who they will become because of what they have been around while you're building your home-based business. Your children understand what goal setting is and

> Did you know that a $5,000 one-time investment made at a child's birth by parents and grand-parents grows to $2,560,000 by the time the child is 45 years old?

working for something: being in business for yourself, being a self-starter, getting yourself going in the morning when there is not a boss standing over your shoulder and you go do it anyway. It's about the recognition you receive, who you become, what you learn about yourself, and how you give back to the world. The education you receive from your business is the best to empower yourself and other people. What we discovered when we got involved in our business, was that we could empower parents to become better people and better parents. Better people empower their children. We believe that encouraging the entrepreneurial spirit is the answer to building self-esteem in children in our world."[26]

At age 11, Justine started her own business offering small books to manage business cards. She has learned several important lessons: how to balance her checking and savings accounts, how to make deposits and withdrawals, that 70 percent of every dollar goes back into the business to keep it functioning, and how to get up in front of a networking meeting to make a presentation. It was a momentous day when she finally took all of her profits and purchased a Nintendo DS. Since it wasn't a gift, that DS meant significantly more to her because she earned it. When seeing how much money Justine was earning, seven-year-old Andrew asked how he could start his own business.

> *Many times children come up with their own business ideas, and it's very important that parents support and uplift that entrepreneurial spirit.*

The opportunity to start a promotional-button business for network marketers crossed our path, and he jumped at the idea. He took on a significant business loan, opened his own banking accounts, made hundreds of buttons, and earned a very big Lego set that he wanted. In spite of the earnings, Andrew's interest in his business waned, and we were in a constant battle with him to make buttons when orders came in. In our discussions about calculating profit, we learned that Justine had to work fifteen minutes to make four dollars whereas Andrew worked approximately two minutes to make four dollars. As a result, Justine was very interested in purchasing Andrew's business since he was no longer interested in it. He agreed that her purchase price would be taking on the financial responsibility of the remainder of the loan payment. Many people would think that these concepts were far too advanced for children, but our experience has revealed the opposite. With a little extra information and the patient understanding that this was their first exposure to business tasks, they understood everything.

Many times children come up with their own business ideas, and it's very important that parents support and uplift that entrepreneurial spirit. Your children will need a lot of your love and patience because you will be asking them to learn new, difficult skills. Help your children dream bigger so when the potential order for 1,000 units comes in, they are mentally prepared. Tell them that the whole family will pitch in and that they can even hire their school friends to help. Even if you think their business ideas won't work, help them as much as you can. And if the idea doesn't pan out, tell them about Thomas Edison's 10,000 successful attempts at figuring out how not to build a light bulb. Tell them that they just figured out what business to stay away from and that they will figure out a bigger, better, more profitable business. They just have to find a need and fill it. Who knows; your children may have the next million-dollar idea!

Spread the Fertilizer

Earlier in this chapter, Orrin Hudson mentioned, "It's all about giving." When you are holding on to every penny, the Universe understands that money is a scarcity in your life. When you give money to other's who need it more, it tells the Universe that you have more money than you need, so the Universe continues to give you more.

On every convenience store's counter sits a smudged paper cup with the words "Take a penny, leave a penny" or some variation of the phrase. Do you take more than you leave? Those pennies may seem insignificant to you, but they potentially mean the difference between eating and going hungry for others. In Chapter Five, we mentioned that little things mean a lot. In the realm of giving, this is especially true. Even the smallest gift can change someone's life. Those television commercials of children walking through a slum in some third-world country come to mind. Only 75 cents a day changes the lives of these children. Pocket change to us means life to others.

As we travel along the path in life, we strive for success. Our focus is primarily on pursuing our dreams and desires. Our focus is on finding what it is that we want and setting **Ask and you shall receive.** goals to achieve it. We won't argue with anyone on the importance of this. You have to know exactly what you want for your life and then go after it with all your energy. But there is another aspect of accomplishing this that may seem counterintuitive: giving. We know this may not make sense. You work, save, and plan for your dreams, and we're telling you to give away your hard-earned resources. This is imperative if you want to live an abundant life.

> One of the greatest gifts is giving. Several years ago, while we were waiting for church to begin, we overheard a young woman chatting with her friend in the pew behind us. She was talking about how little money she had, and then she said, "How am I supposed to give money to the church if I can't even pay my electric bill?" It took a lot of will power to not turn around and tell her she had it backwards.

Until you give freely of what you have, you'll never gain any more. This isn't a religious concept, either. This is universal. All successful people understand and practice giving.

We believe the spirit of generosity comes from a person's value system. At the very core of who we are is a willingness to give: to share our gifts, talents, knowledge, and resources with others. It is a beautiful thing to give without thought of getting something in return. And yet, giving without some thought of balance can be destructive. A person who has truly mastered the gift of generosity of spirit gives in ways that are healthy for both the giver and the receiver.

Giving and receiving mixed together can inspire others when they have the opportunity to do the same. That is the balance that we are talking about: giving can incorporate time, skill sets, energy, knowledge, or material things. It doesn't matter what you give; what is important, however, is being aware of the needs of others around you. Be willing to sacrifice a little of what you have been blessed with to benefit others. Do you know someone who can benefit from what you have to offer? Giving completes the circle of life.

> There are so many real-life examples of this. Pull any personal development book off the shelf, and chances are good that you'll find the example of Henry Ford and his persistence. He isn't the only Ford who should be commended, though. His son Edsel is an example to us all in the world of philanthropy. In 1936, Edsel established the Ford Foundation with an initial gift of $25,000. This foundation has grown into a national and international philanthropy dedicated to the advancement of human welfare with annual donations exceeding $550 million.

Imagine how many individuals the Ford Foundation has helped. How would our world be different if Edsel hoarded his family's fortune? How many young people are in the world today just waiting for a scholarship to college? What if, with our help, one went on to become a doctor and find the cure for cancer or diabetes? How many lives would be saved; all because you made the decision to choose to give? These questions may seem a bit overly altruistic, but the truth of the matter is, donating your time, money, resources, or energy benefits the planet.

Giving allows us to accomplish things far beyond ourselves, and that is part of what living the life of our dreams is all about, right? With this gift, our accomplishments are through not only us but through others as well. We are here on earth not simply to survive; we're here to thrive. Life isn't about survival of the fittest. Instead, it's about people from all walks of life living in unity and harmony for the mutual benefit of all.

The best way to create more income without requiring you to work more hours is to create multiple sources of income (MSI) as your financial foundation.

Plant Variety

Can you imagine planting one bush in your yard and expecting that one little bush to prevent erosion like a lush lawn would? No, you wouldn't. Think of your income earning potential like your yard; it needs a large variety of plants and trees. How do you increase your income? The most obvious way is to work more hours at the job, but remember how we talked about the problems of trading time for money? In Chapter Three, we talked about needing a blueprint to determine where you want to go in life. The best way to create more income without requiring you to work more hours is to create multiple sources of income (MSI) as your financial foundation. The wealthiest portion of the population does not earn all of its income from one job or even one business. Their income comes from a wide variety of businesses and investments.[5]

Think about a skyscraper. These giants stand firm and strong over the streets below, but how do they stand so tall without falling down? Their foundation is carefully designed to support them just as the foundation of your MSI should be carefully designed to remain strong and consistent. A good deal of thought and effort has been put into the foundation of a building, and your financial foundation should be the same.[5]

Once a strong foundation is built, the construction of multiple sources of income is easy. If we equate a skyscraper as financial freedom, then this is like seeing your wealth rise high into the sky because the stronger the foundation, the more stories of wealth you can add!

You may wonder what it means to set up multiple sources of income that flow in on an automatic and consistent basis. We will talk more on this subject later in the chapter, but with multiple sources of income, you won't have to work much more than usual to create additional sources of income. You don't have to endure struggles or hardships to increase your income. The key is to view your income-earning potential differently. Believe, and you will achieve.[5]

Most of us only have one source of income—our current job. Unfortunately, our job never seems to provide us with the amount of money we need to live the life we dream about. But what if you had all the money you desired? One of our first goals was to get a check in the mail every day. Imagine walking to your mailbox and finding it filled with money. This is very possible when you have multiple sources of income.

> *Create a habit by making sure your children understand that a portion of every dollar they earn is theirs to keep today and into the future.*

What does the phrase "multiple sources of income" mean? It means exactly what it says—income from many sources. This is fairly straightforward, but what is meant by "sources" of income? If you and your spouse both have jobs, then does that mean you are getting multiple sources of income? Perhaps a two-income family could be classified as one that has multiple sources of income based on the fact that there is more than one income, and they do bring a steady flow of money into your bank account. But that isn't really what we mean when we talk about MSI. An MSI includes things such as real estate, network marketing, Internet businesses, joint ventures, and various other types of investments. An MSI delivers money to you on a regular basis without you having to show up to work every day. With an MSI, you make money even when you are sleeping.[5]

The Universe is overflowing with MSI opportunities; you just have to tune into them and not dismiss them when the thoughts come to you. Here are a couple of ideas to help you tune into your creativity:

- What do you love to do?

- Is there something you always wanted to do but didn't know how to make it happen?

- Have you had an idea about a product or service that you didn't act on?

- What do people tell you that you are good at?

- When you think of multiple, change it from two to many more (50, 100, 200).

- Change your thought of steady income from once a month to multiple times a day.

An important aspect of an MSI is that you want to create "passive" sources of income as often as possible. We don't believe that trading time for money is the most efficient way to earn it, so any form of income you receive shouldn't take a lot of your time or energy to maintain once it has been established. Your goal is to create an environment where you receive money on a regular basis because you contributed in some way but aren't actively involved on a daily basis. Having said that, we want to remind you that you don't get something for nothing, so you will have to spend some time and energy in the beginning setting up the MSI so that it works on autopilot. The amount of time it takes depends on the MSI, but after the start up phase, your MSI will continue to earn you money without your direct involvement.

Another important point to remember regarding an MSI is that everyone is a contact. No matter who the people are, they could be an important connection in realizing a potential source of income for you. Don't jeopardize a potential contact through inappropriate actions. Remember the Golden Rule: do unto others, as you would have them do unto you. You should be professional in all of your dealings. You never know; the cashier at the grocery store may be a critical piece for a source of income in the future. You are making all kinds of contacts and talking to people every day who could potentially help you or give you ideas for more MSIs. Maintain those contacts, and be sure to keep the relationships positive.

An MSI delivers money to you on a regular basis without you having to show up to work every day. With an MSI, you make money even when you are sleeping.

Don't worry about being perfect. All you have to do is give it the best you've got. Every day, give it your best effort. Dare to live the life you have imagined. Visualize exactly how you want to live, then take steps, no matter how small, toward having that life. Don't view an MSI as something that's going to happen in the distant future; instead, look at it as something that already is. The earlier you teach children about the value of money, the more likely they will be prepared for the financial ups and downs of adulthood. Teaching your children about our complex financial system may seem daunting, but you can help put your child on the right track by instilling the right thought process in them now.

Let's take us, for example. This book will create royalties, we work with a network marketing company with life-changing health benefits, and we are in the process of setting up several Internet businesses and joint ventures.

Now it is time for you to do some brainstorming. In the space below, start making a list of ways to make money. Be creative and get beyond your limiting beliefs. Creativity is an important aspect concerning MSIs. Don't concern yourself with what others are doing; try something new that has never been done before. Use the space below to list new and creative ways to make money (don't think only in terms of MSI's either).

WAYS TO MAKE MONEY

1. _____
2. _____
3. _____
4. _____
5. _____
6. _____
7. _____
8. _____
9. _____
10. _____

For more writing space please visit
www.ParentOutLoud.com/STEP to download your free Play-Book.

Proper Maintenance

Effective parents take full control of their lives by eliminating the negative influences. And if they're swimming with the sharks, they find another pool. Happiness is not an accident. It is a deliberate, systematic process of deciding where you want to go and what it will look like when you get there. You then have to follow your plan and take the necessary steps toward making that plan become a reality.

Less successful parents, unfortunately, are those who continually dwell upon their problems, sit on the sofa exhausted, watching TV all evening, and pass their problems and beliefs on to their children. Successful parents are those who continually work to better themselves and fill their minds with images of the people they would like to be and the lives they would like to lead. They also make a conscious choice every day to impart that knowledge to their children. This is a responsibility that falls solely on the shoulders of the parent; it just can't be taught in school. But what an exciting responsibility, because teaching your children how to be successful in all areas of their life is extremely rewarding and fosters deeply connected relationships with your children.

We've covered a lot of new concepts in this book; how your beliefs are formed, the Seven Levels of Awareness, the Eight Natural Laws of the Universe, your Six Higher Faculties, the effect of negative energy on you and your children, how to change your attitude, goal setting and attracting an abundance of many riches in your life. These are important concepts that many adults never learn, so imagine the incredible gift you will provide your children by teaching them these concepts at a young age when their minds are so open to soak up the knowledge and understanding. These concepts are not something that you impart by sitting down and having a family meeting; they are woven into the daily conversations and teaching moments you have with your children. For example, when one of our boys has a meltdown because he waited all day to empty the dishwasher, it's a perfect opportunity to discuss the Law of Cause and Effect. His choices set in motion the new effect that he would not only have to empty the dishwasher, but he would also have to fill it with the dirty dishes on the counter.

As you incorporate this new knowledge into your life, you will be modeling for your children how to handle various situations. A really important one for Anamarie has been to acknowledge out loud that she is "consciously aware of being in a negative vibration," and they watch her turn on uplifting music or chose an activity that helps her get in a better mood.

Our hope is that you have not only read this book, but you have highlighted phrases, marked up things that are light-bulb moments to you, made notes in the margins and added sticky flags for easy reference. Take a few minutes every day to read through a few paragraphs and let the information soak in to you. Let it become part of you and in time you will have made amazing strides toward expanding your Awareness Level, deepening your sense of Peace, and creating a family that you thoroughly enjoy.

ACTION STEPS

Listen to the way you talk about money and write down any negative references you may use. To the side, change those references to positive statements.

Start your money jars.

> Adults: 10% FFA, 10% EDU, 10% Give, 5% Play, 15% LTSS, 50% Necessities

> Children: 10% FFA, 10% EDU, 10% Give, 10% Play, 10% Gift, 50% LTSS

Create an MSI for the family to work on together.

For more writing space please visit www.ParentOutLoud.com/STEP to download your free PlayBook.

IN CONCLUSION

What type of legacy do you want to leave? We invite you to take the next "step" and join our Six-S Team of Empowered Parents (STEP). We're always accepting new members! Please visit our website for a free Six-S Family PlayBook, featuring all of the Action Steps in this book with additional space for you and your family to create your dream life. You will also be able to gain access to over 30 hours of phenomenal parenting advice from our expert interviews and learn about products we've created to make parenting more enjoyable. We're here to help you "parent out loud," because *what you say does matter*. Please visit www.ParentOutLoud.com today.

ACKNOWLEDGMENTS

We'd like to thank Bob Proctor for following his passion of teaching people how the mind works. This opened our world to discovering our passions and pushing ourselves through our terror barriers! We'd also like to thank Liz Ragland for her assistance and wonderful support and our amazing MasterMind groups for their priceless, brilliant ideas throughout the whole process. We are eternally grateful to our final editor, Lynda Masterson, and her cheerful willingness to edit again, and again ... and again.

A special word of appreciation to the phenomenal parents we interviewed and the life-changing wisdom they provided. All of you fueled our fire to be better parents by expanding our awareness even further. We would also like to acknowledge each other for the support and encouragement we gave to one another throughout the process.

And finally, we would like to thank you, the reader, for having the interest to pick up this book and the personal desire to complete the exercises to change your life to reflect the greatness within you. Through our journey of personal growth, we know that passing on what we've learned will make a difference for the future generations of the world.

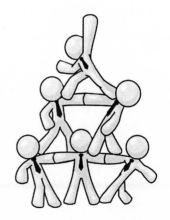

What You Don't Fix ... Your Kids Inherit

KEY PARADIGMS

CHAPTER 1

❖ Paradigms are the governing belief systems that determine our success in life and as a parent. We learned many of our paradigms from our parents, which is why it is so important to *change the beliefs* that aren't serving us so that we don't pass them on to our children.

❖ We cannot attempt to change someone else, including our own kids if we don't *change ourselves first*.

The first six years of your child's life, are very influential because that is when they are ingrained with the mindset they carry for the rest of their lives.

❖ As parents, it is important for us to realize that our children are incredible and unique. We are **responsible** for molding these young minds and melding them into the people they ultimately become.

❖ Our *paradigms control* our current behaviors and lives. Change them and you can change your life!

❖ More often than not, people are unhappy and lack fulfillment because they don't know how to unlearn their outdated beliefs. In some cases, they may not even understand what the problem is.

❖ Our children are an extension of us and if we don't like their behavior, we need to start by *looking at ourselves.*

❖

CHAPTER 2

❖ A family must be one tight unit, not two; it's not the parents versus the children. Every family member needs to feel that his or her **home is a sanctuary** from outside life.

❖ Every **decision** you make *affects* something in your child's life.

❖ You can at this very moment make a conscious effort to change your thoughts and give your children a lasting legacy of *happiness and security.*

❖ Our *Mind* encompasses every cell of our body and is responsible for our higher functions such as reasoning, thought, and memory and has the capability to expand beyond our physical body. *It is part of the infinite energy of the Universe.*

❖ Our children are just little human beings, who lack *life experiences* and depend on us to teach them.

Your subconscious mind is like software for the mind; it's running all of your programs. To change our thoughts and habits, we have to change our software.

❖ Free-will resides in our conscious mind. It can accept or reject any idea.

❖ The conscious mind reads and interprets the stimuli taken in from our five senses: sound, sight, taste, touch, and smell.

❖ Our **subconscious** has no ability to reject any idea or thought; it **simply accepts** every suggestion made to it.

❖ A child is born with empty conscious and subconscious minds. **A child's subconscious mind is like a sponge.** It soaks up everything with which it comes into contact.

❖ Our subconscious mind is a culmination of our past experiences and memories. It is also where our habits and belief systems are formed. It consists of memories, which have an emotional connection to the past.

❖ If you want to know what you are *thinking* subconsciously, simply *look* at your child's results.

CHAPTER 3

❖ Teach your children that **they can do anything** they want to do, that they can accomplish anything they want to accomplish.

❖ Any thought you *impress upon the subconscious mind repeatedly* becomes fixed in part of your personality.

Renewing or shifting from your current thoughts to those that you desire brings about transformation and change in your life.

❖ Your attitude is reflected in your **self-image**, which comes from your thoughts, feelings, and actions.

❖ Focus on what you do want and you will **attract** that to you.

❖ Part of developing **Emotional Intelligence** in our children is to give them a broad range of *words* for their feelings.

❖ What we **think** about our children, whether we say it out loud or not, it is **impressed** upon them from a very young age.

❖ We all are inherently good and meant for **greatness**. It is just a matter of whether we choose to *believe* so.

❖ If you fill your mind with thoughts that influence positive behavior, you will take positive actions and therefore achieve positive successful results.

❖ Our children are just as **intelligent** as us. They only lack life experience.

CHAPTER 4

❖ We have to **decide** to change our beliefs. Doing so automatically equips our children to live in their future, not our past.

❖ Not only can you have the life you've always dreamed of but you can give your children the tools to build the life of their dreams as well.

❖ If we want to improve the results in our children's lives, we not only have to change our thoughts, we also have to increase our Level of Awareness.

❖ The next time you feel yourself starting to react to a situation, *stop for a moment*; think about the ramifications of your actions before letting your survival instincts take control.

❖ **Great** people talk about *ideas*. **Average** people talk about *things*. **Small** people talk about other *people*.

❖ *Life is about learning.* It is a journey and we don't stop developing after we are out of school.

❖ There is no one else like you in this world and you were put here for a purpose.

❖ **Each** child has to wake up to the **truth** of who they are within.

We have no control over what others think and it is none of our business anyway.

❖ We can teach our children to **let their diamond sparkle** early on and continue into adulthood so that the world will see how amazing they are, what gifts God gave them, and to live into their potential.

❖ There has to be a distinct separation between parenting and friendship. Many parents want their children to like them. **Liking** you and **respecting** you are entirely different.

❖ **Pay attention** and become aware of your feelings, behaviors, words, and thoughts that you are feeling, doing, and saying, especially around your children.

> **The opinions of others such as your parents, spouse, co-workers, or friends don't matter. Only your opinion truly matters.**

❖ As you become more aware of your actions, you will begin to move up the Awareness Levels toward **Mastery**.

❖ Throughout our lives our identity has been strongly influenced by society.

❖ What is truly important to us, to our deeper, true self, comes from the answers to "What have I done that I will be proud of at the end of my life? What **legacy** will I leave to my children?"

❖ If our children spend too many years acting like someone else, they soon *forget* that they are pretending.

❖ What society says doesn't matter. You are the **ruler** of your life.

❖ A person is successful if they are ***pursuing a worthy goal or ideal.***

❖ It is your **purpose** that keeps you going and striving for your goals despite the obstacles that may come in the way.

❖ Your past and your possessions do not define you. Let go and move forward with a realistic, ***confident belief in yourself.***

❖ Why are you here on this planet? What **gifts** have you been given that you can give back to the world?

❖ **Visualize your dream**, define it, and then go for it! Choose to be happy and share that happiness with the world.

❖ There is nothing more influential, to your children than for them to see you **passionately** engaged in something you love.

❖ If all of your expenses were covered, how would you fill your days?

❖ ***Success*** is something we can *learn, master* and *teach* our children.

CHAPTER 5

❖ Do you know what *your* children really *want*?

❖ The Natural Laws of the Universe are the ***unwavering and unchanging principles*** that rule our entire Universe and are the means by which it continues to thrive and exist.

❖ Parents who teach their children the Natural Laws of the Universe **prepare them for success.**

❖ A firm **understanding** of the Natural Laws of the Universe is a distinguishing factor between reaching your dreams by **accomplishing** your goals and living a life of mediocrity.

❖ *We become what we think about.* What is our thought but energy?

❖ Once you start to align your actions and thoughts with these Laws you can begin to **attract** and **experience** outcomes that you used to think were impossible.

Research indicates that along with Einstein, many of the great scientists were raised in an environment that taught them in thousands of ways that there are Natural Laws in the Universe and that those Laws are to be respected.

❖ Any situation can look good or bad depending on what it is compared against.

❖ The images you **hold** in your mind most often will materialize in your life.

❖ Once you've memorized a picture in your mind and continue to reinforce the image, *it moves into form* with and through you. This is how thoughts become physical objects.

❖ It is just as easy to **dream big** as it is to dream small, so why dream small?

❖ **Everything is relative.**

❖ You teach children how to judge whether something is good or bad in your life by **your reactions.**

❖ Our perception is what *shapes our world* into what we see and experience.

❖ Your children **are a mirror of you.**

❖ If you so choose, you can **think positive thoughts**, which lead to **positive vibrations** and will in turn put you into a **positive mood.**

❖ You can only attract that which is in *harmony* with your chosen vibration. Bad moods attract negativity. *Great moods attract an abundance of good.*

❖ God does not give us a bad situation without also giving us the seed of an equivalent benefit.

❖ It is important to realize that we aren't going to feel great all of the time, no one does. If we did, would we even know when we were happy?

❖ *Luck, chance, and accidents don't exist.*

❖ In each area of your life, develop *positive statements* you can repeat in your mind regularly. It is through repetition that we replace old habits of thoughts with new, positive thought habits.

When you're looking for gold, you go through tons of dirt, but you don't focus on the dirt, you focus on the gold!

❖ Remember, sometimes we think a door is shut because we have done something or something has happened to us that we perceive to be negative. That is the *cause.* You get to control the *effect.* **You get to control** what happens on the other end.

❖ You must have **faith** that your ideas and goals are moving into physical form.

❖ Just having the knowledge of how the Natural Laws of the Universe operate will be of no benefit to you unless you *consciously work with them.*

CHAPTER 6

❖ Our Intellectual Faculties give us the ability to think, transform, and **create** the life we desire.

A Dream/Success Journal is a special journal where you write all your successes and achievements.

❖ Just like your physical muscles, your *mental muscles* must be exercised if you are to keep them strong and fit.

❖ We have to reject the old habit and consciously work to replace it with a new habit we want.

❖ Never underestimate the role of *Perception* in our daily lives.

❖ Part of what our job is as a parent is to *show our children all of the sides of a situation* which we can see, but that they have not yet learned to understand through personal experience.

❖ When you are using your **reasoning** skills, you will quickly reject anything that doesn't match your current understanding or paradigms.

❖ Many spiritual leaders have said that prayer is "us speaking to God" and *intuition* is "**God speaking to us.**"

CHAPTER 7

❖ Gauge your success based on your own life.

❖ *Self-esteem* is a major component in determining what we consider to be success or failure.

❖ One *negative* comment has been proven to be *17 times* more powerful than a positive comment.

Our Values determine our Perception of what is right and wrong, good and bad.

❖ *Values* are the defining factors that determine whether or not we succeed.

❖ **Train your mind** to find out where you are and where you want to get to by striving to be the best you can.

❖ Our Values determine our **Perception** of what is right and wrong, good and bad.

❖ The next time that someone's actions upset you, ask yourself, "Which of my rules were broken? **Why do I react the way I do?**"

❖ Another person's rules for values and acceptable behavior can be different than our own and that is okay.

❖ We can **be infinitely greater tomorrow** than we are today.

CHAPTER 8

❖ **Attitude** is a composite of your thoughts and your feelings and your results. All you need to do with a child to help them change their attitude is to tweak just one little part of their thoughts.

Refusing to forgive someone is like taking poison and expecting the other person to die.

❖ Our **thoughts** create our *feelings*. Our **feelings** create our *actions*. And our **actions** create our *results*.

❖ We often don't give ourselves sufficient credit for all we've accomplished, particularly when we encounter difficulties in life.

❖ Your **attitude** is more important than your *aptitude* in determining your success in life.

❖ Focus on what *is* working and what you *do* want.

❖ Question everything with "**Is it true?**" You will be astounded with how many things in your life really aren't true.

❖ We have the power to flip our own switch and *choose the altitude of our attitude.*

❖ The more personal growth you do as an individual, the *happier* you are, the more *fulfilled* you feel, the *better* your life works. You are a happier person to be around. Your kids feel that.

❖ We all have talents, gifts, and uniqueness. Our obligation is to accept these gifts and spend our lives sharing our gifts with our children and the world.

CHAPTER 9

❖ When your parents don't believe in you, then you start not believing in you. When your parents don't tell you, "**I love you**," that hurts the self-esteem of the child. A lot of children don't grow up with hugs.

❖ Why is it that we'll spend hundreds or thousands of dollars on physical workout equipment but not a single penny on *mental workout equipment?*

❖ Thomas Edison *failed* over 10,000 times when inventing the light bulb, but when he was asked about his failures, he responded, "**I have not failed**, I've just found 10,000 ways that won't work."

The next five and ten years are going to happen whether or not you set goals. The odds are pretty high that without goals you will be in a very similar place as you are in now.

Put ideas on paper and literally begin to paint the picture of how you want your life to be. In turn, your children will want to paint the picture of their life.

❖ We have learned that one of the best methods to teach your children to prepare for the future is to set *goals*.

❖ Goals that don't challenge you move you sideways, not forward. You need to get out of your comfort zone and force yourself to **learn new and difficult skills**.

❖ You have to be **looking for the clues from the Universe** because they never come with a neon sign.

❖ It is critical that you spend time *visualizing* yourself *achieving* your goal.

❖ We can't set a goal bigger than our paradigm until we **believe** in ourselves.

❖ Earl Nightingale says, "Success is the *pursuit* of a worthy goal."

❖ Every day we need to ask ourselves the question: "Am I getting any closer to my true definition of success in life? Am I making this world a better place to live?"

❖ **We become what we think about.**

❖ What we create in our lives we create from our thinking. Everything that exists in this world came about because someone thought about it.

❖ Believing is *Seeing*.

❖ Scientific research has proven that your subconscious can't tell if something is real or imagined and your subconscious is where your beliefs are held.

❖ Because *thoughts are vibrations*, your thoughts actually affect people and your environment.

❖ For *visualization* to be effective you must use all of your senses and put as much *emotion* into it as you can.

❖ A journal of **gratitude** helps to increase your awareness of how blessed you are in life.

CHAPTER 10

❖ The most important thing to teach your children is that they are no better than anybody and they are no worse than anybody.

❖ Replace "We can't afford it" with "**Yes**, we could purchase that, but today we're **not choosing** to spend our money that way.

❖ You must *acquire the habits* and skills of managing a small amount of money before you can have a large amount.

Create a habit by making sure your children understand that a portion of every dollar they earn is theirs to keep today and into the future.

❖ Teach your children that *the Universe is unlimited* and that if they truly believe, it is possible to have any amount of money they desire.

❖ **Ask and you shall receive.**

❖ We can learn from our children. They live by the principle that *it never hurts to ask*...and ask, and ask.

❖ Benjamin Franklin once said, *"An investment in knowledge always pays the best interest."* Answering your children's questions honestly and in terms they'll understand can help them begin life on sound financial footing.

❖ Did you know that a $5,000 one-time investment made at a child's birth by parents and grandparents grows to *$2,560,000* by the time the child is 45 years old?

❖ The best way to create more income without requiring you to work more hours is to create Multiple Sources of Income (MSI) as your financial foundation.

❖ Multiple Sources of Income deliver money to you on a regular basis without you having to show up to work every day. When you have Multiple Sources of Income, *you make money even when you are sleeping.*

BIBLICAL AND BOOK REFERENCES

Collins, James. *As a Man Thinketh.* "Law, not confusion ..." p. 27.

Law of Perpetual Transmutation

Wattles, Wallace. *The Science of Getting Rich.* "There is a thinking stuff ..." p. 18.

Psalms 37:4–5
Matthew 21:22
Romans 12:2
James 1:5-6

Law of Relativity

Numbers 13:18-20

Law of Vibration

Isaiah 41:10
Mark 11:23
Luke 11:34; 12:27–32
1 Corinthians 15:33
Philippians 4:11-12

Law of Attraction

Matthew 7:7; 21:22
Luke 11:9-10

Law of Gender/Gestation

Ecclesiastes 3:1
Romans 8:25

Law of Polarity

Genesis 8:22
Psalm 74:16-17

Law of Rhythm

Psalms 46:10
Proverbs 10:28
Philippians 4:11-12
James 1:2–3

Law of Cause & Effect

Proverbs 11:27; 14:22; 17:13
Matthew 6:4; 12:33-37
Luke 6:43
Galatians 6:7
James 4:8

INTERVIEW CREDITS

1. Alex Karis—HurricaneOfGratitude.com
2. Andrea Samadi—SecretForTeens.com
3. Anjila Stimack
4. Annie Fox—AnnieFox.com
5. Bob Proctor—BobProctor.com
6. Cherrie St. Germain—MyTruMind.com
7. Chris Miles—FireYourFinancialAdviser.com
8. Chris Souchack—Shwoof.com
9. Dave Albano—FullLifePotential.com
10. Deena Morton—SixMinutesToSuccess.com
11. Denny Hagel—InnovativeParentingLLC.com
12. Doug Miller—CoachDoug.com
13. Ed and Leah Severance
14. Elizabeth Ragland—TagPublishers.com
15. Felicia Miller
16. Gary Malkin—WisdomOfTheWorld.com
17. Grace Keohohou—DSWA.org
18. Holli Walker—BeyondTheSecretTeachers.com
19. Kirsten Nelson—ParentingByTheMinute.com

20. Leanne Gerrard—AwakenedGrowth.com

21. Leigh Scott—LeighMScott.com

22. Les Brown—LesBrown.com

23. Leslie Householder—JackrabbitFactor.com

24. Lisa Walker—LisaWalker.org

25. Marsha Jacobson—MarshaJacobson.com

26. Nicki Keohohou—DSWA.org

27. Orrin Hudson—BeSomeone.org

28. Patrick Calliari

29. Peggy McColl—PeggyMcColl.com

30. Rebeka Karrant

31. Roxie Griego

32. Sarah Robinson—Escaping-Mediocrity.com

33. Shabana Ahmad—IntegrityHumanCapital.com

34. Stephen M.R. Covey—SpeedOfTrust.com

35. Rev. Wendy Craig-Purcell—WendyCraigPurcell.com

36. Jewel Seidel

SOURCE CREDITS

37. Amzi Griego Marsh

38. Elle Raunston—MotivateMe.info

39. Mary Morressey—MaryMorressey.com

CPSIA information can be obtained at www.ICGtesting.com
261459BV00001BA/1/P

9 780986 776236